RECORDED VERSIONS
GUITAR

AUTHENTIC TRANSCRIPTIONS
WITH NOTES AND TABLATURE

Los Lonely Boys

Music transcriptions by Steve Gorenberg and David Stocker

ISBN 0-634-08907-2

HAL•LEONARD®
CORPORATION

7777 W. BLUEMOUND RD. P.O. BOX 13819 MILWAUKEE, WI 53213

In Australia Contact:
Hal Leonard Australia Pty. Ltd.
22 Taunton Drive   P.O. Box 5130
Cheltenham East, 3192 Victoria, Australia
Email: ausadmin@halleonard.com

Visit Hal Leonard Online at
www.halleonard.com

Señorita

Words and Music by Henry Garza, Joey Garza and Ringo Garza

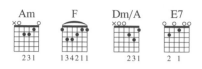

Tune down 1/2 step:
(low to high) E♭-A♭-D♭-G♭-B♭-E♭

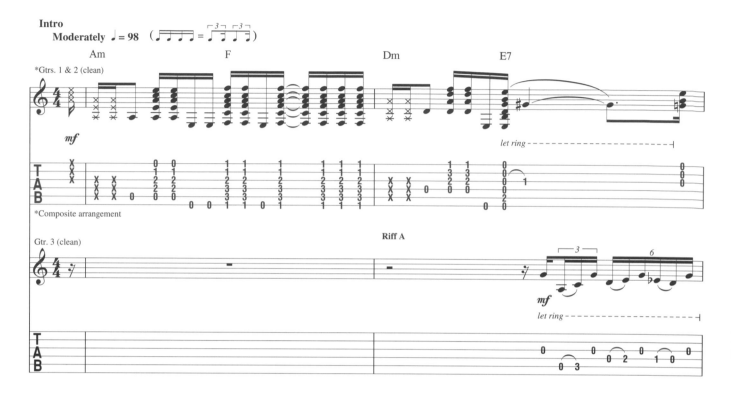

*Composite arrangement

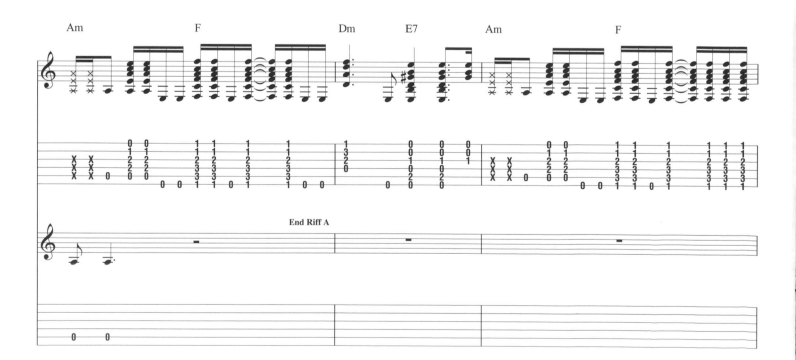

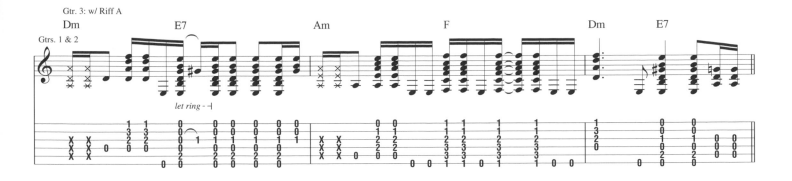

Well, let me tell you, ba - by, your mom-ma did-n't raise no fool. ___

let ring

End Rhy. Fig. 1

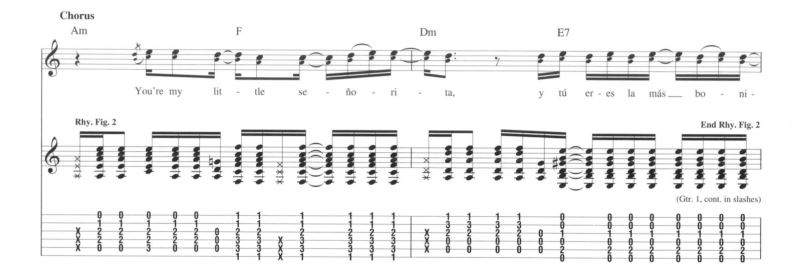

Chorus

You're my lit - tle se - ño - ri - ta, y tú er - es la más ___ bo - ni -

Rhy. Fig. 2

End Rhy. Fig. 2

(Gtr. 1, cont. in slashes)

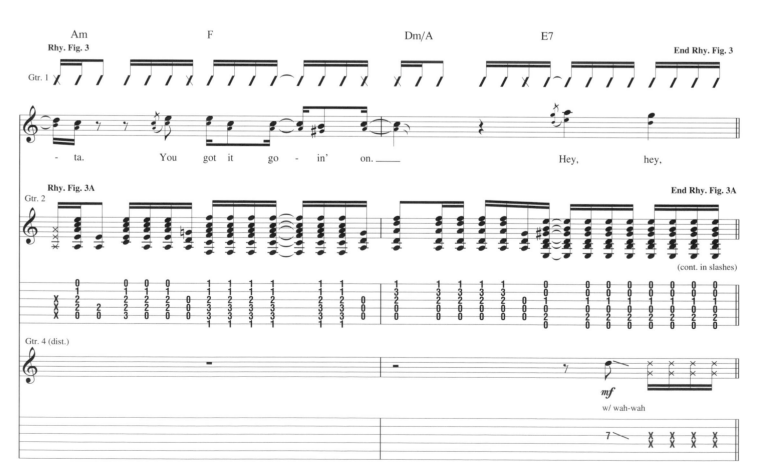

Rhy. Fig. 3

Gtr. 1

End Rhy. Fig. 3

- ta. You got it go - in' on. ___ Hey, hey,

Rhy. Fig. 3A

Gtr. 2

End Rhy. Fig. 3A

(cont. in slashes)

Gtr. 4 (dist.)

mf

w/ wah-wah

Guitar Solo

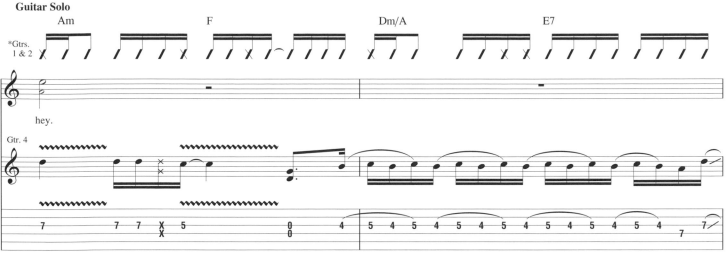

*Composite arrangement

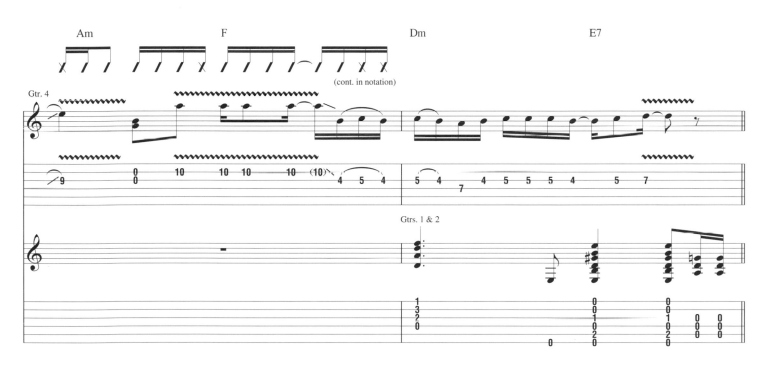

Verse

Gtrs. 1 & 2: w/ Rhy. Fig. 1
Gtr. 4 tacet

2. Mom - ma warned _ me 'bout _ a girl _ like you, _

(Do, _ do, do, _ do, do, do,

she said, "A girl like that _ is gon - na break your heart _ in two." _

do.)

With her sex - y legs _ and hair _ and nas - ty look - in' walk, _

(Nas - ty look - in' walk.)

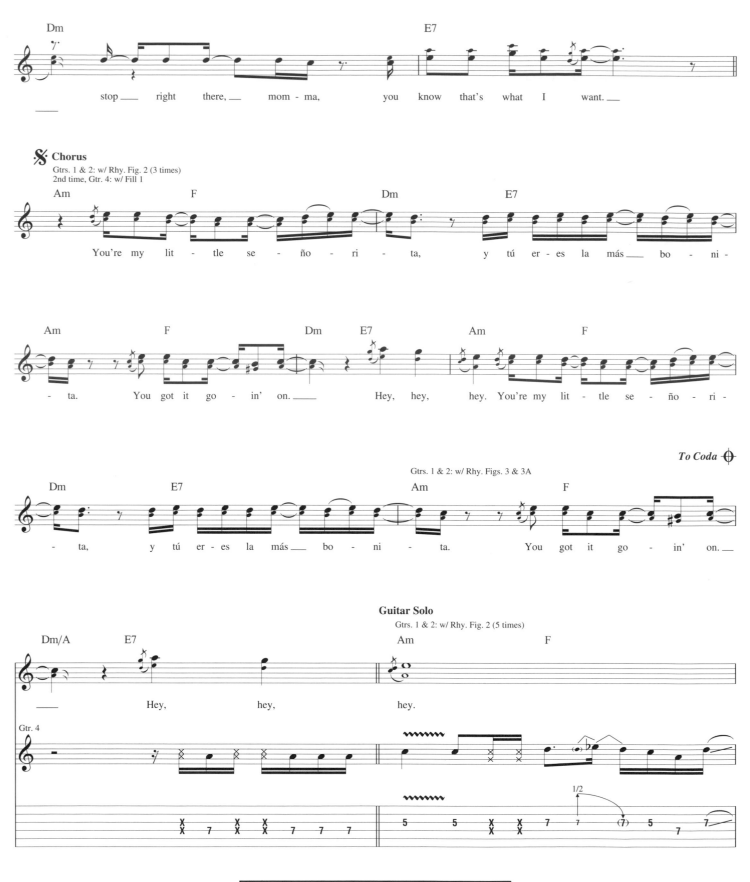

stop ___ right there, ___ mom - ma, you know that's what I want. ___

Chorus

Gtrs. 1 & 2: w/ Rhy. Fig. 2 (3 times)
2nd time, Gtr. 4: w/ Fill 1

You're my lit - tle se - ño - ri - ta, y tú er - es la más ___ bo - ni -

- ta. You got it go - in' on. ___ Hey, hey, hey. You're my lit - tle se - ño - ri -

To Coda

Gtrs. 1 & 2: w/ Rhy. Figs. 3 & 3A

- ta, y tú er - es la más bo - ni - ta. You got it go - in' on. ___

Guitar Solo

Gtrs. 1 & 2: w/ Rhy. Fig. 2 (5 times)

___ Hey, hey, hey.

Gtr. 4

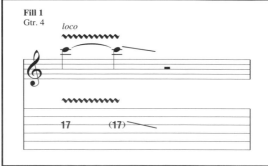

6

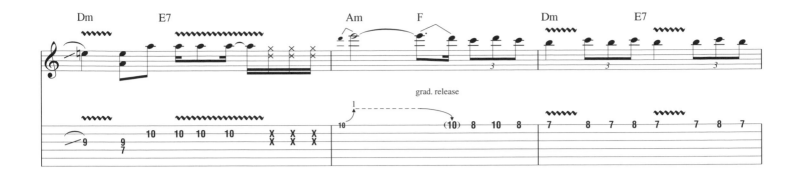

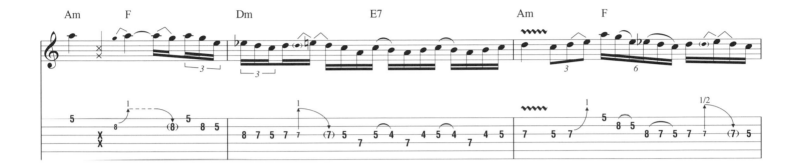

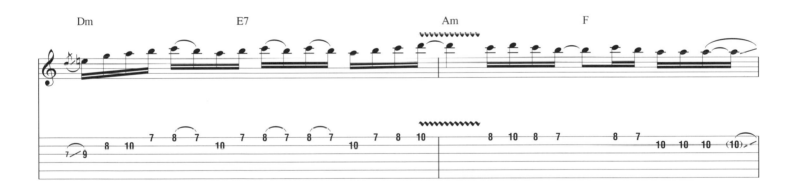

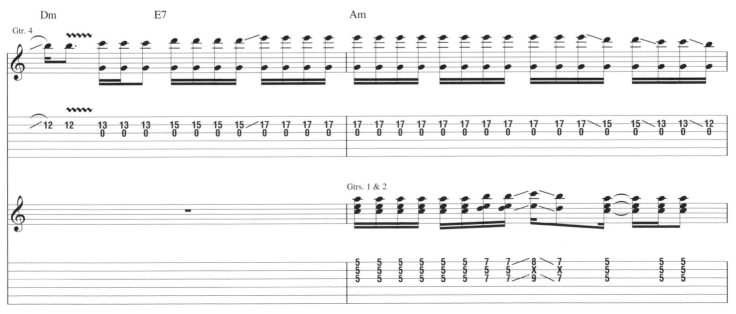

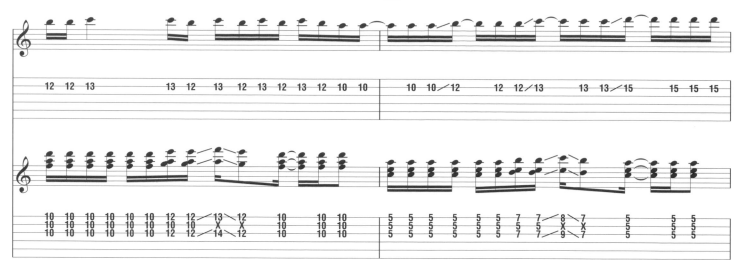

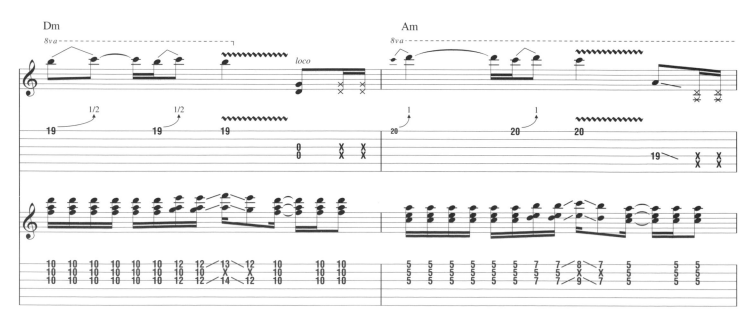

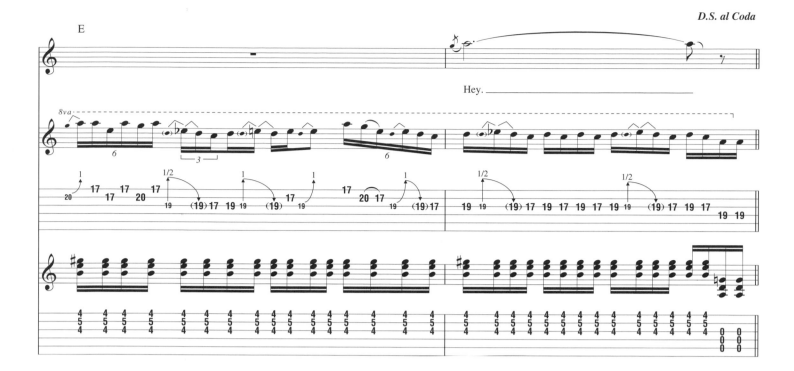

Coda

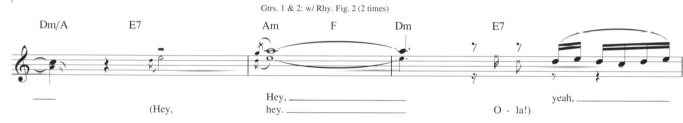

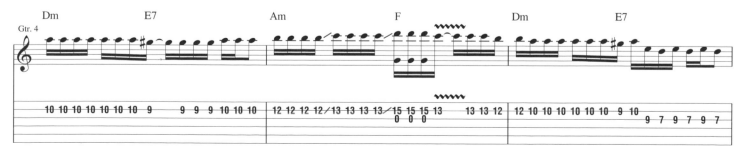

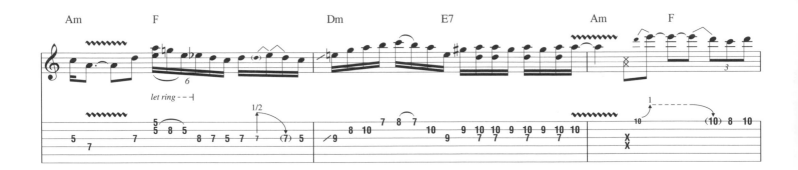

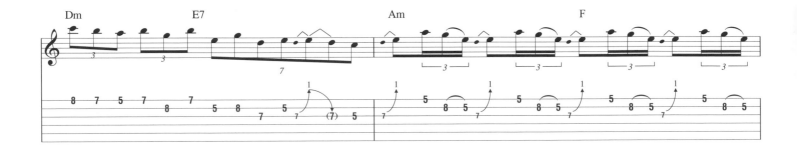

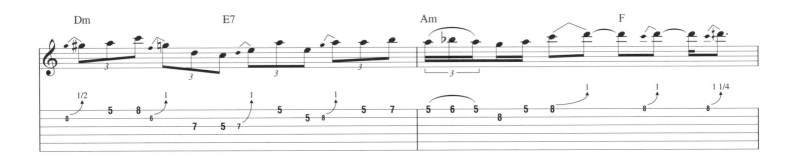

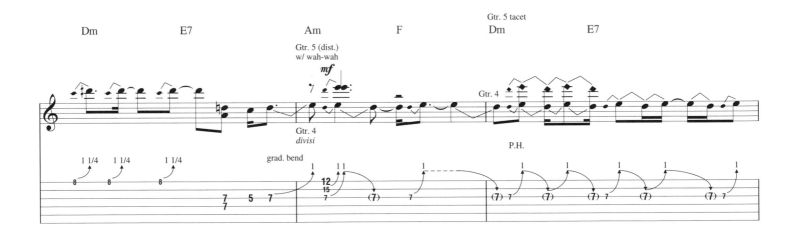

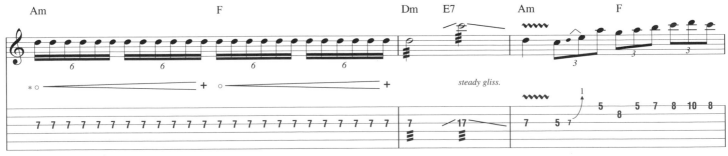

*○ = toe up, + = toe down

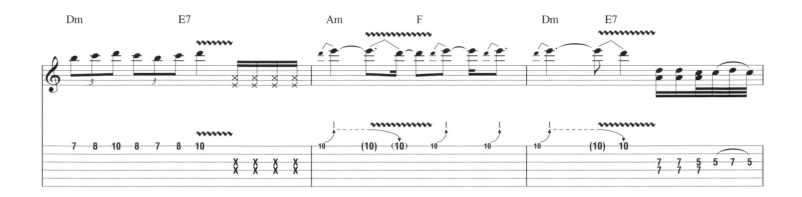

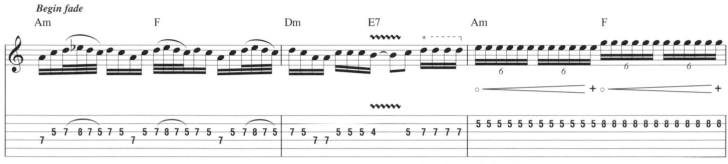

*Played as straight sixteenth-notes.

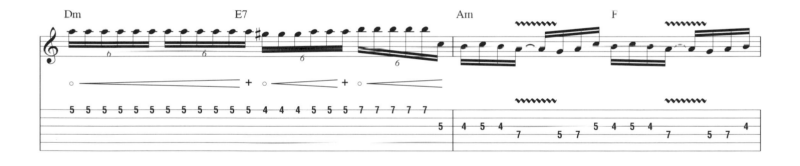

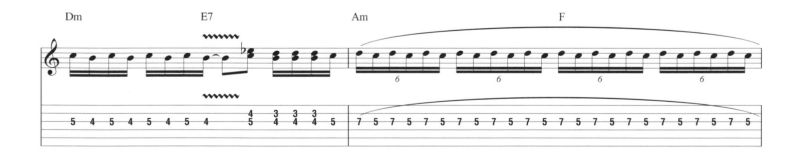

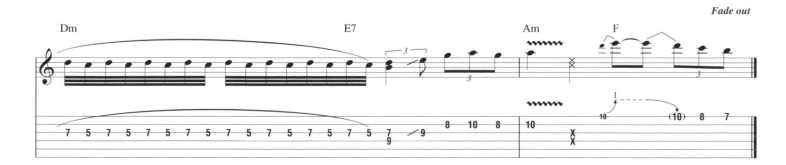

Heaven

Words and Music by Henry Garza, Joey Garza and Ringo Garza

Tune down 1/2 step:
(low to high) E♭-A♭-D♭-G♭-B♭-E♭

Intro
Moderate Rock ♩ = 91

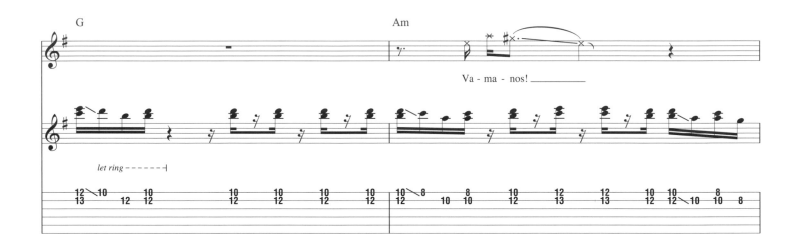

*Chord symbols reflect implied harmony.

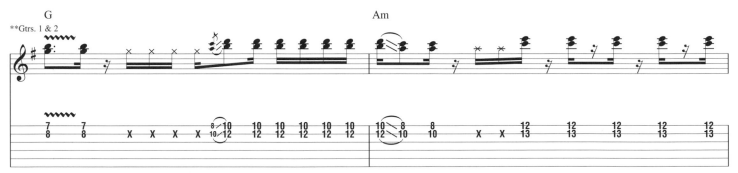

Va - ma - nos!

let ring

**Gtrs. 1 & 2

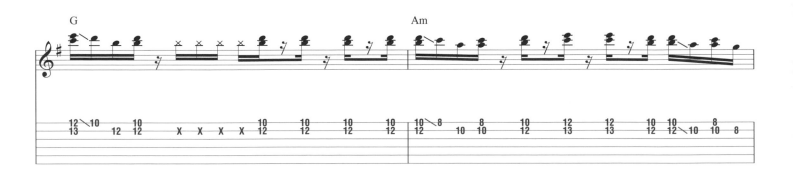

**Composite arrangement, Gtr. 2 (clean) played *mf*.

*T = Thumb on 6th string

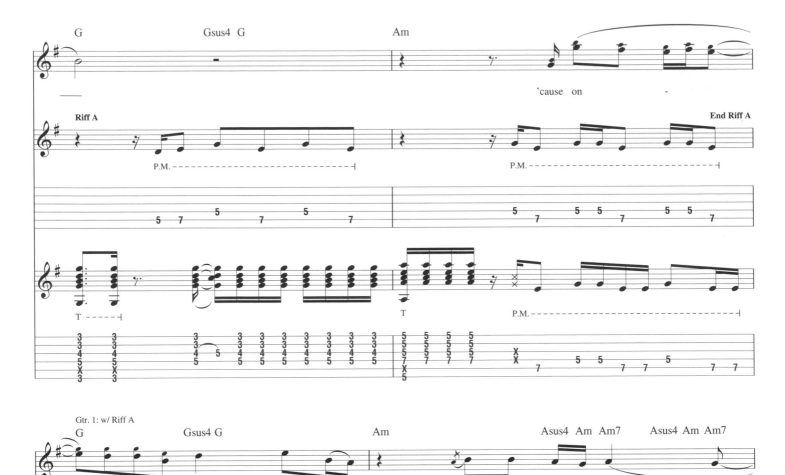

'cause on

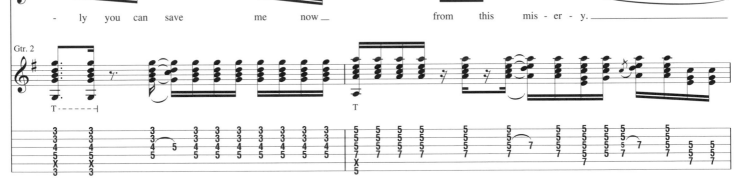

- ly you can save me now ___ from this mis - er - y. ___

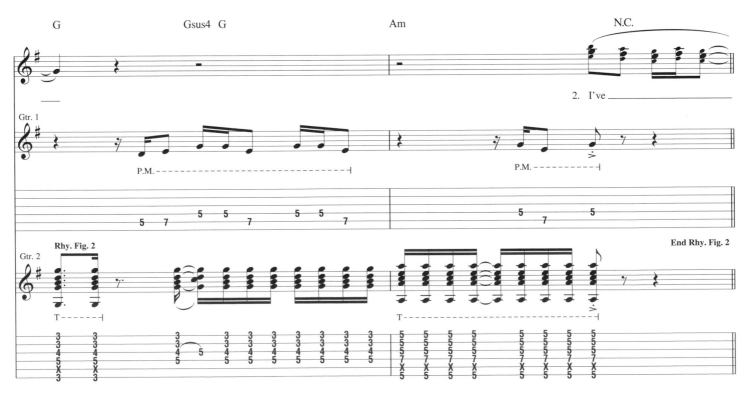

2. I've ___

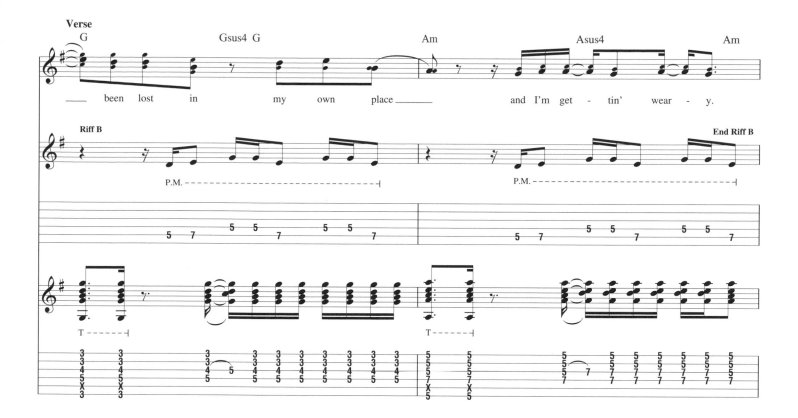

been lost in my own place and I'm get - tin' wear - y.

Riff B

End Riff B

P.M.

P.M.

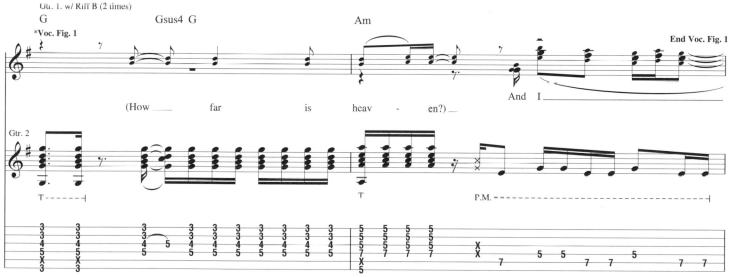

Gtr. 1 w/ Riff B (2 times)

*Voc. Fig. 1

End Voc. Fig. 1

(How far is heav - en?)

And I

Gtr. 2

P.M.

*Applies to upstemmed part only.

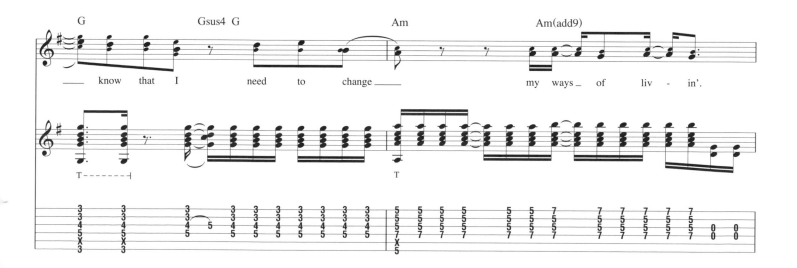

know that I need to change my ways of liv - in'.

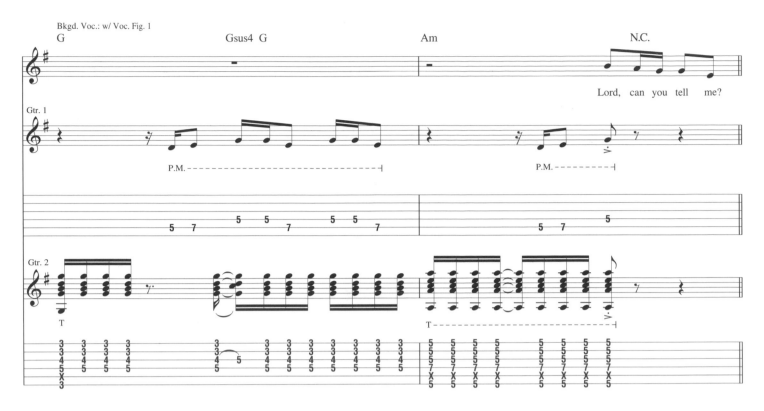

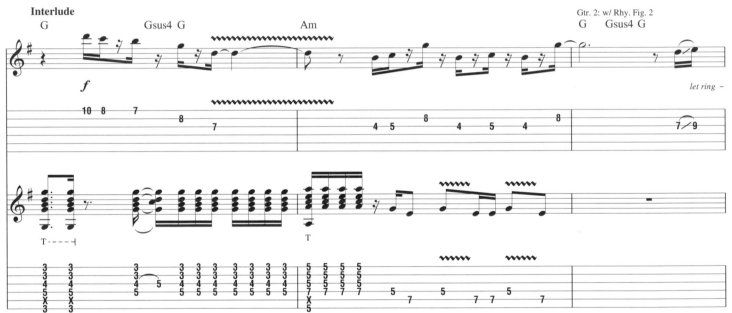

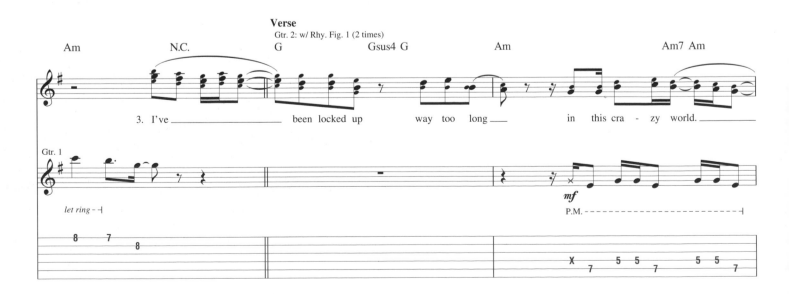

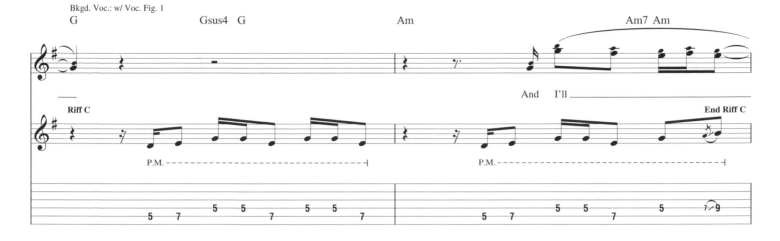

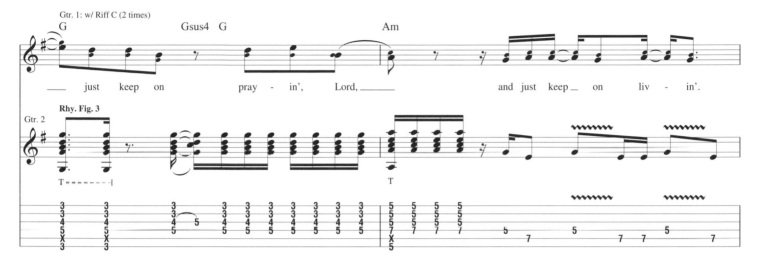

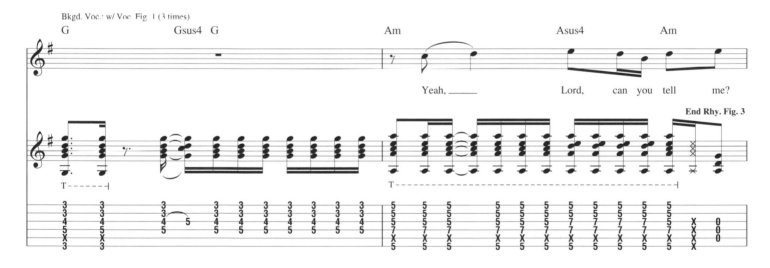

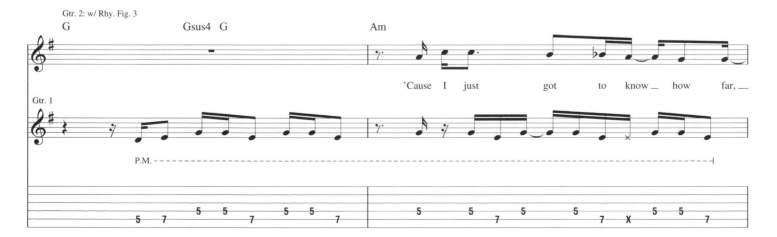

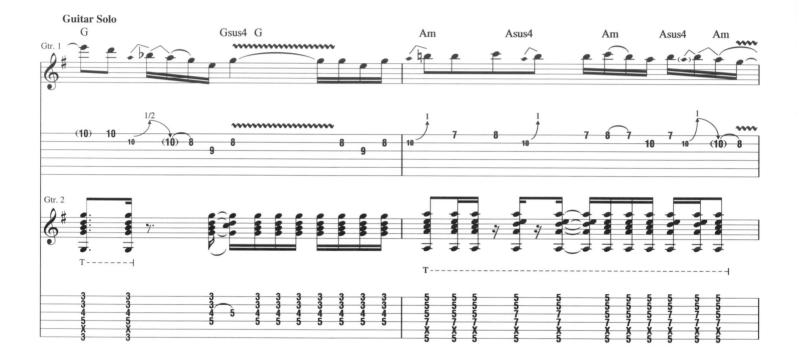

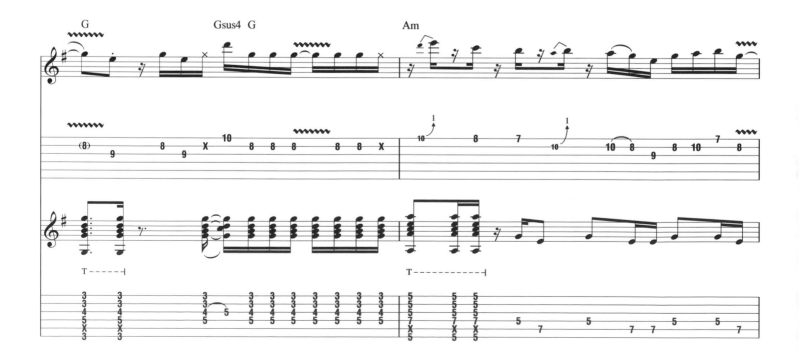

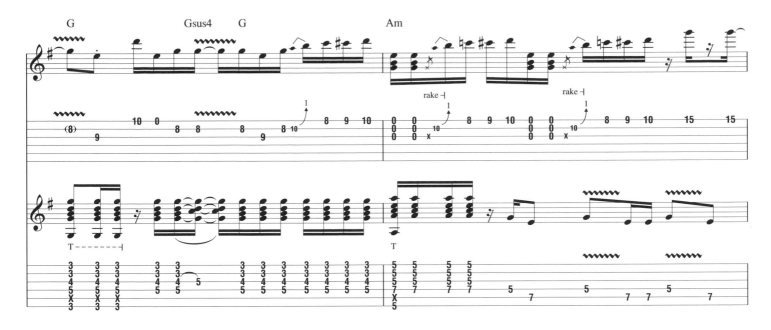

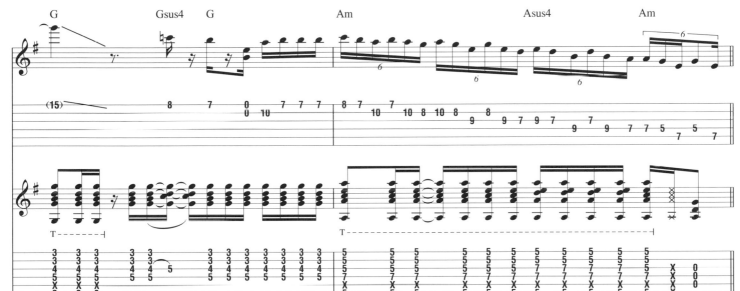

Bridge

Tú que es - tás ___ en - trad - o al ci - el - o, ___

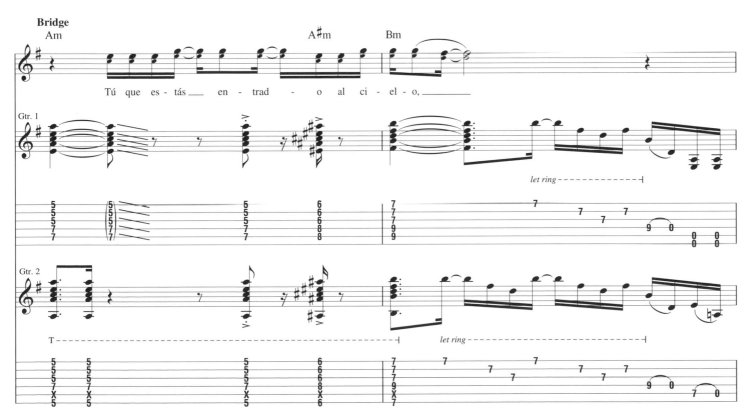

he - cha - me tu ben - di - ci - ón. _____ 4. 'Cause I _____

Verse

____ know there's a bet - ter place ____ than this place ____ I'm liv - in'.

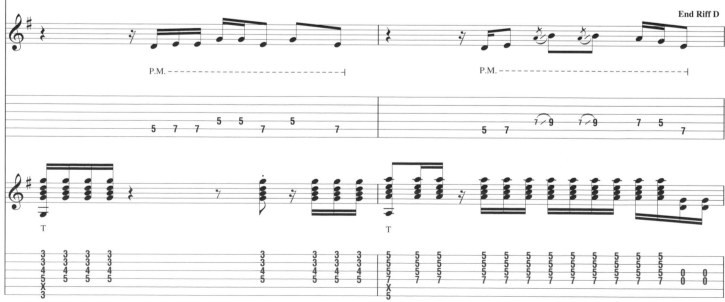

And I _____

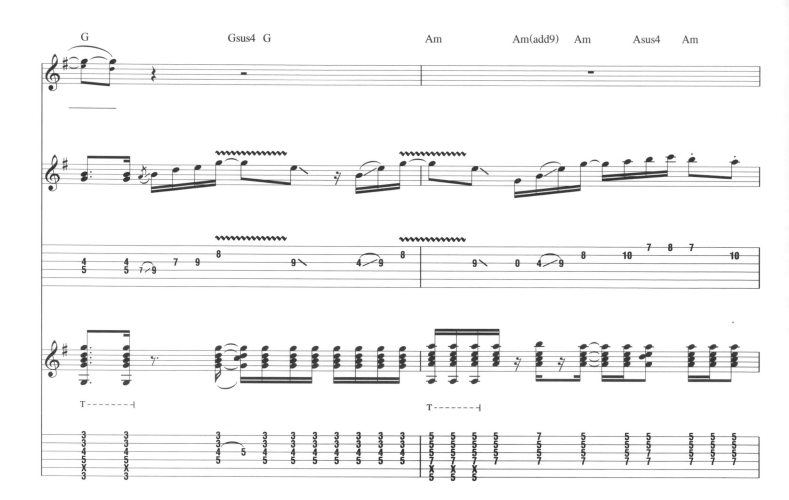

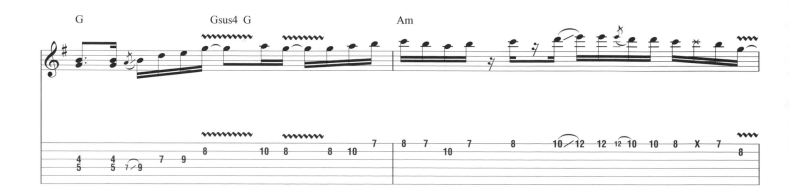

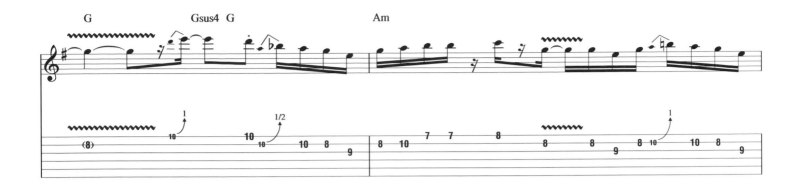

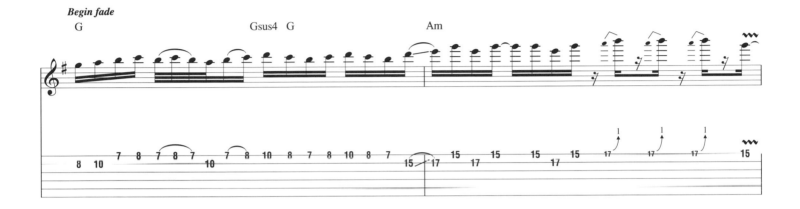

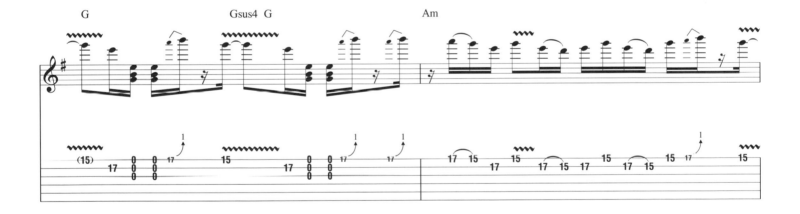

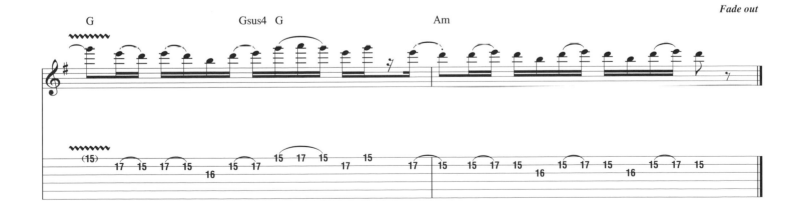

Crazy Dream

Words and Music by Henry Garza, Joey Garza and Ringo Garza

Tune down 1/2 step:
(low to high) E♭-A♭-D♭-G♭-B♭-E♭

Intro
Moderately ♩ = 116

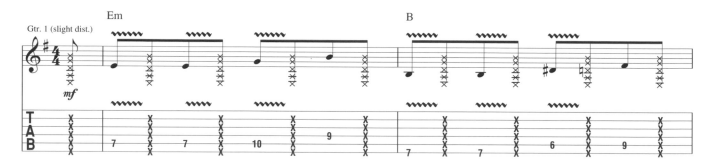

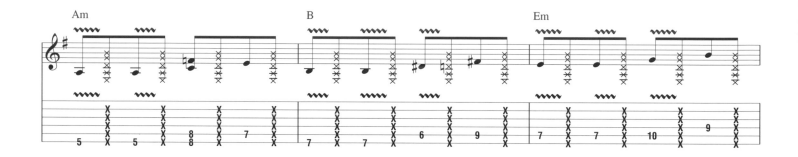

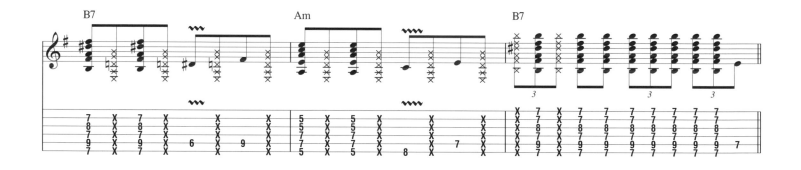

Verse

1. I've tried to find my - self _____ for a ver - y long _ time. _

Rhy. Fig. 1

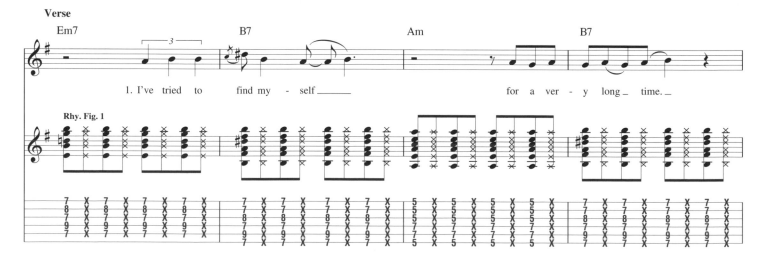

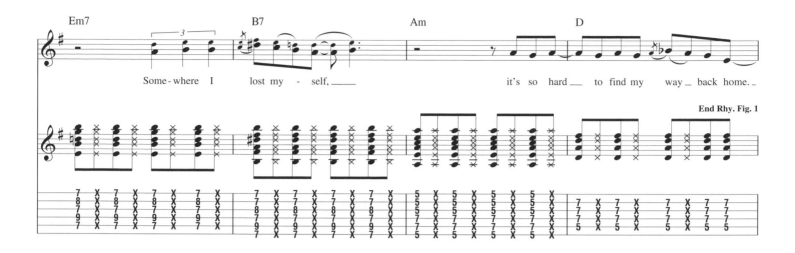

Some-where I lost my-self, _____ it's so hard _____ to find my way _____ back home.

End Rhy. Fig. 1

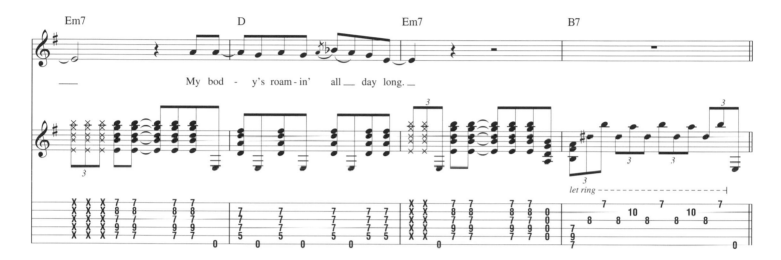

My bod - y's roam-in' all _____ day long. _____

let ring _____

𝄋 Verse

1st time, Gtr. 1: w/ Rhy Fig. 1
2nd time, Gtrs. 1 & 2: w/ Fill 1

2nd time, Gtr. 1: w/ Rhy. Fig. 1 (last 7 meas.)

2. It feels like a real bad _____ dream, _____ I try so hard to break free, _____ yeah. _____
3. A shiv - er in my _____ soul, _____ oh, _____ I think I'm gon-na go.

And e - ven though I _____ try, _____ some-thin' else _____ has got a hold _____ on me. _____
But in the depth of my mind _____ there's a place _____ that on - ly I _____ have seen. _____

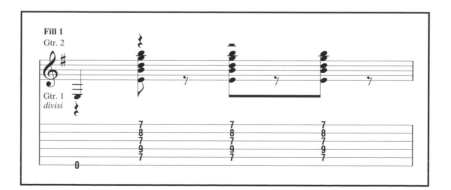

Fill 1
Gtr. 2

Gtr. 1
divisi

Will I ev - er be in con - trol of me?
Will there ev - er be re - al - i - ty?

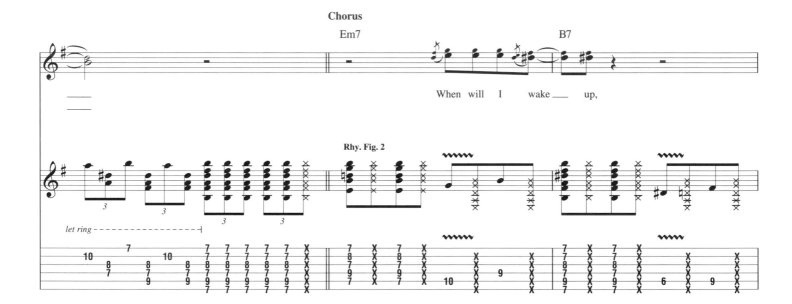

Chorus

When will I wake up,

To Coda

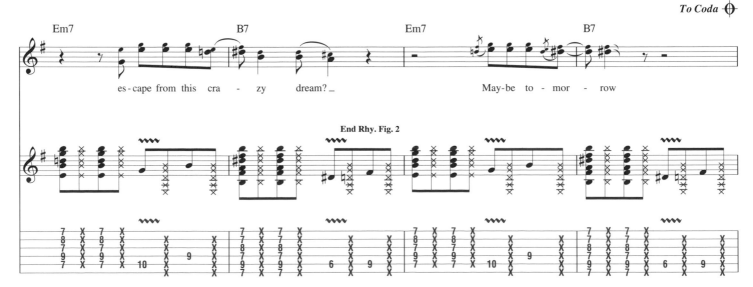

es - cape from this cra - zy dream? Maybe to - mor - row

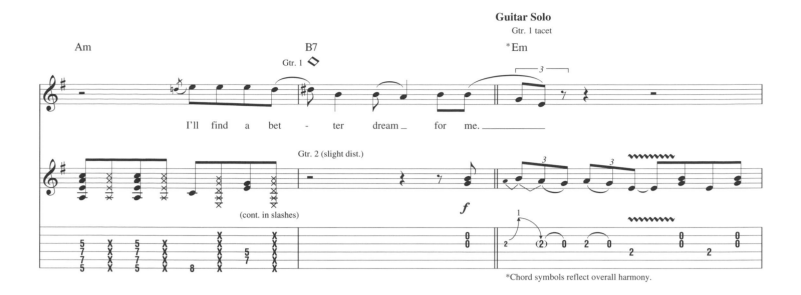

Guitar Solo
Gtr. 1 tacet

I'll find a bet - ter dream __ for me. _____

(cont. in slashes)

*Chord symbols reflect overall harmony.

D.S. al Coda

I'll find a bet - ter dream __ for me. _____

○ **Coda**

Guitar Solo
Gtr. 1 tacet

I'll find a bet - ter dream __ for me. _____

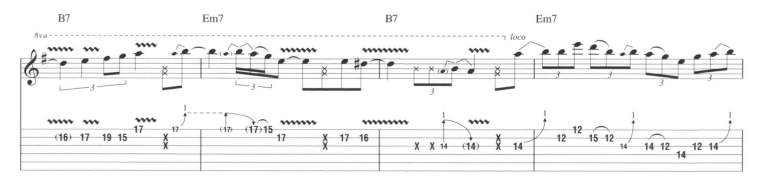

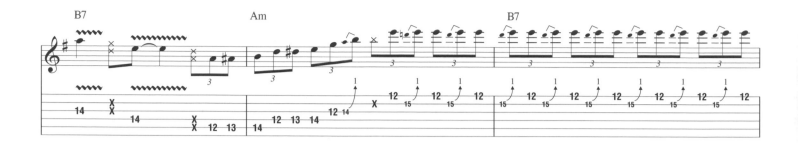

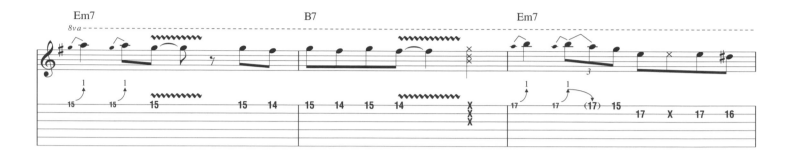

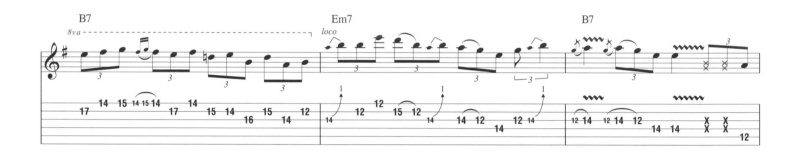

Bridge
Gtr. 3 tacet

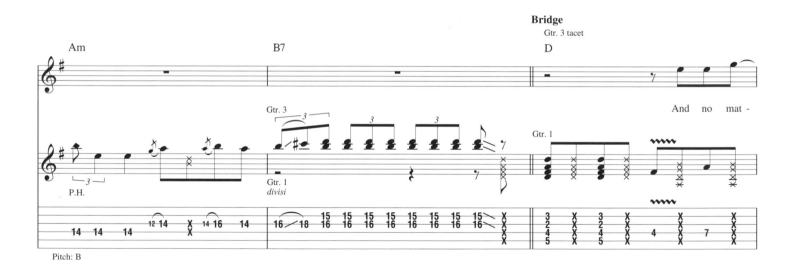

And no mat-

-ter how hard___ I___ try,_____

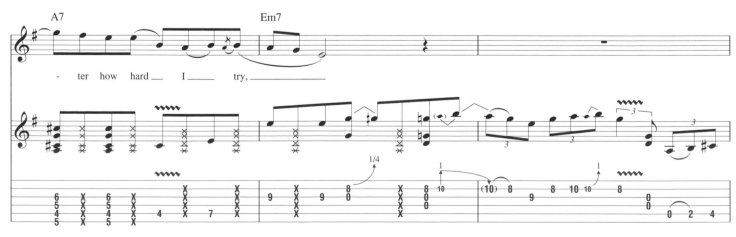

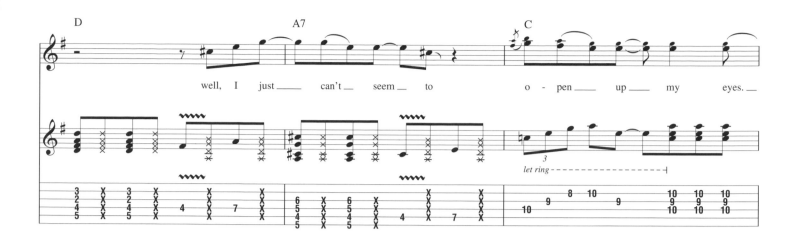

well, I just ___ can't ___ seem ___ to ___ o - pen ___ up ___ my ___ eyes. ___

Chorus
Gtr. 1: w/ Rhy. Fig. 2

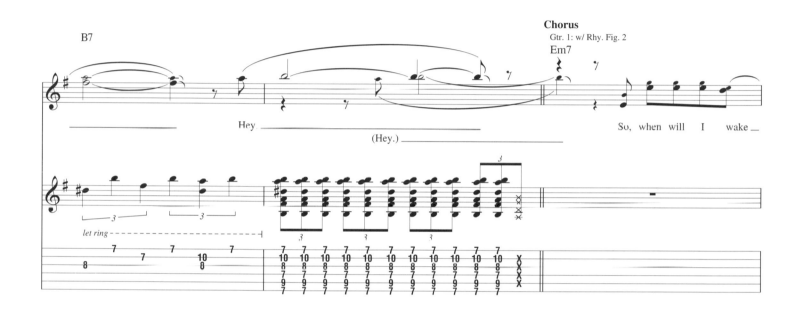

Hey. _____ (Hey.) _____ So, when will I wake ___

___ up, es - cape from this cra - zy dream? ___

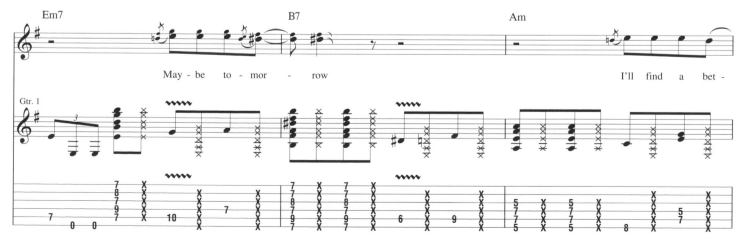

May - be to - mor - row I'll find a bet -

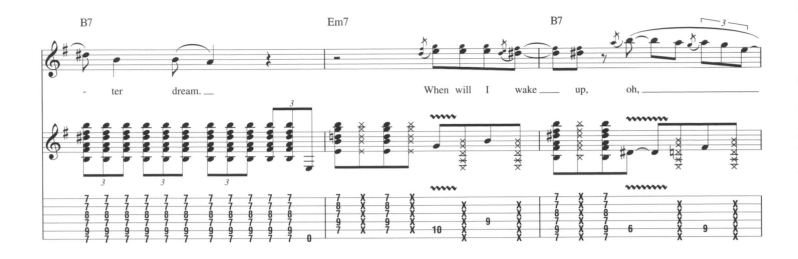

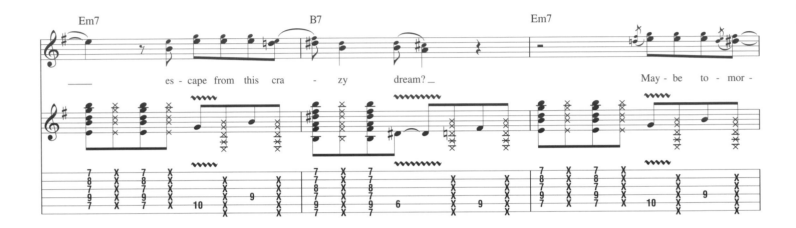

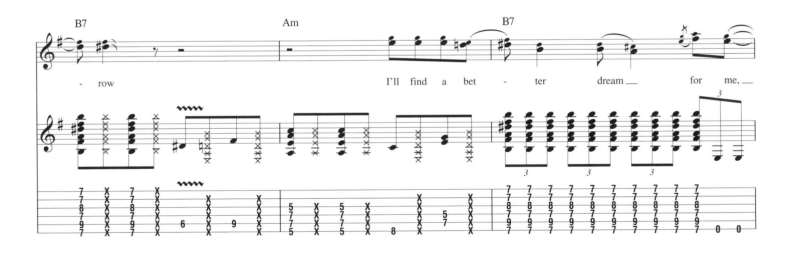

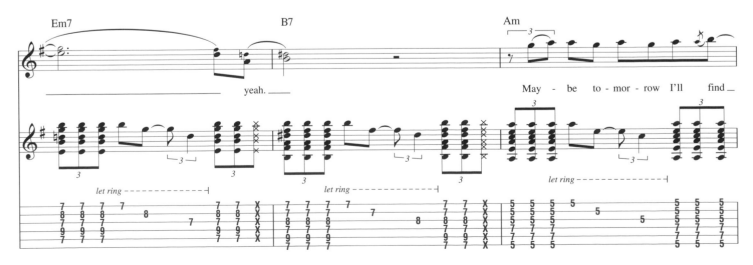

a bet-ter dream, yeah.

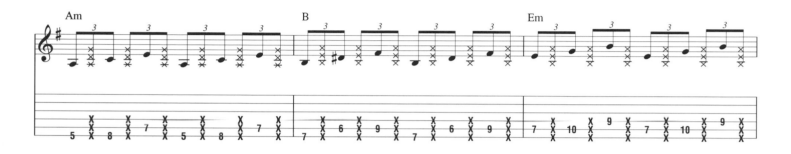

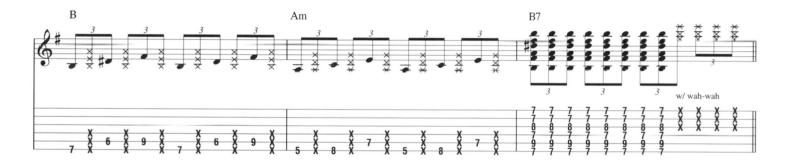

w/ wah-wah

Guitar Solo

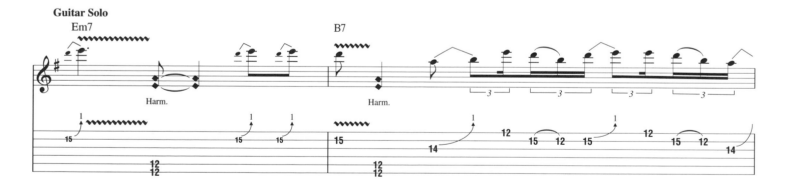

Harm.   Harm.

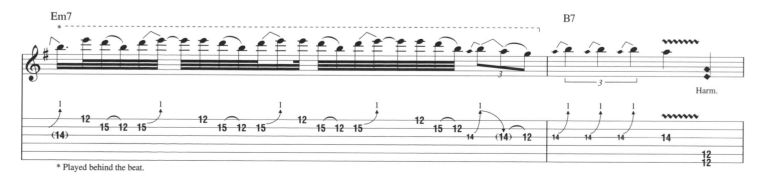

* Played behind the beat.

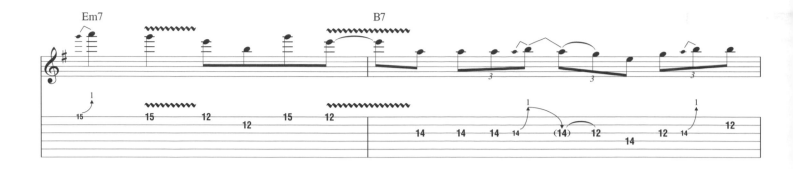

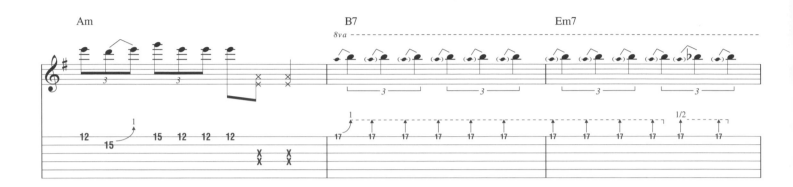

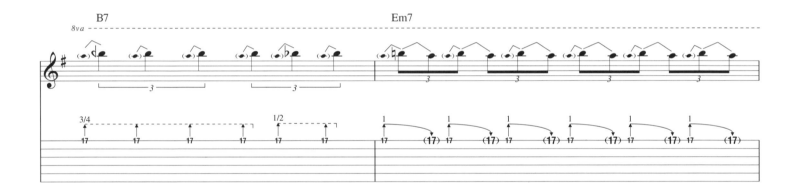

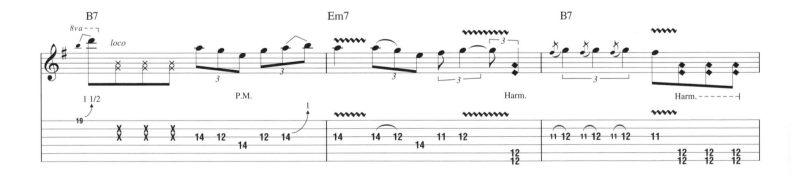

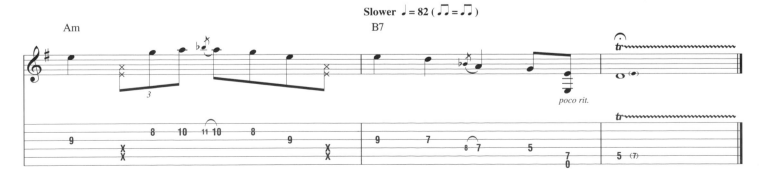

Dime Mi Amor

Words and Music by Henry Garza, Joey Garza and Ringo Garza

Tune down 1/2 step:
(low to high) Eb-Ab-Db-Gb-Bb-Eb

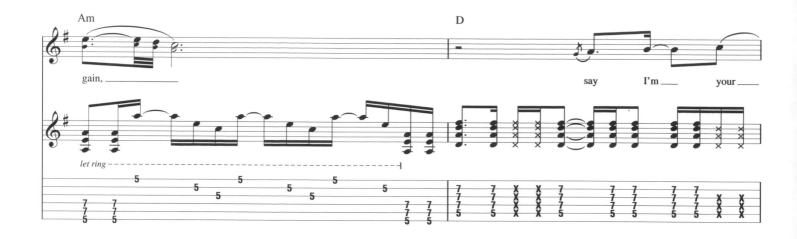

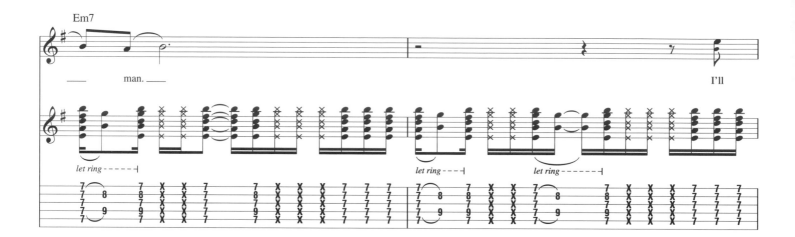

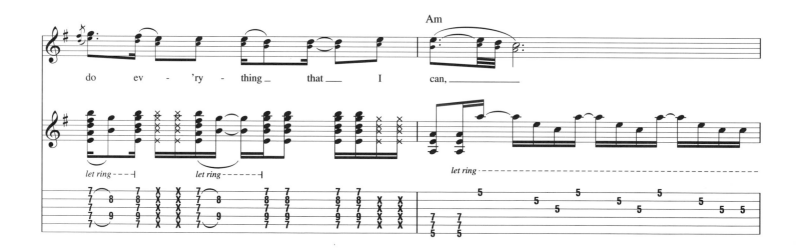

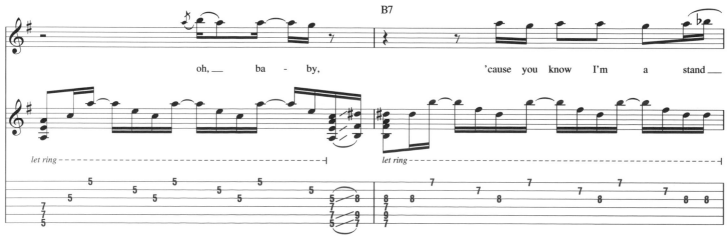

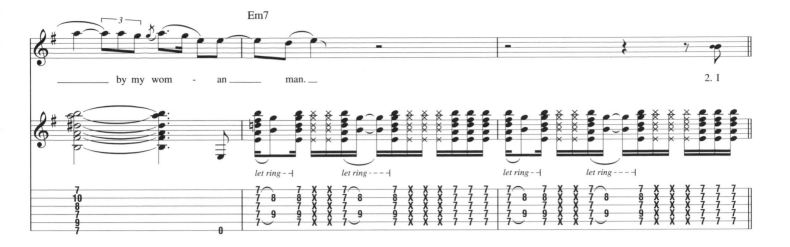

by my wom - an ____ man. ____

2. I

Verse

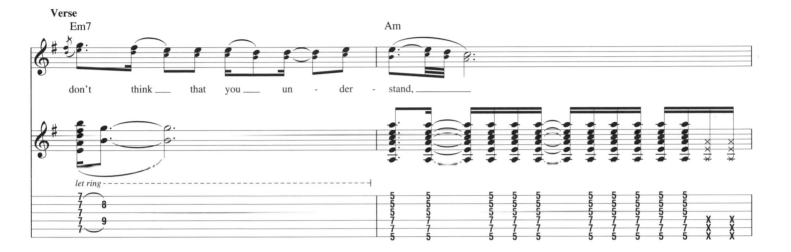

don't think ____ that you ____ un - der - stand, ____

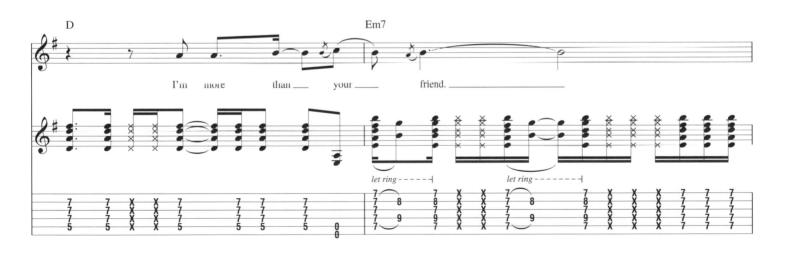

I'm more than ____ your ____ friend. ____

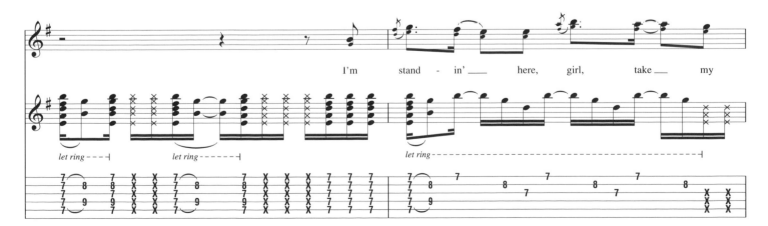

I'm stand - in' ____ here, girl, take ____ my

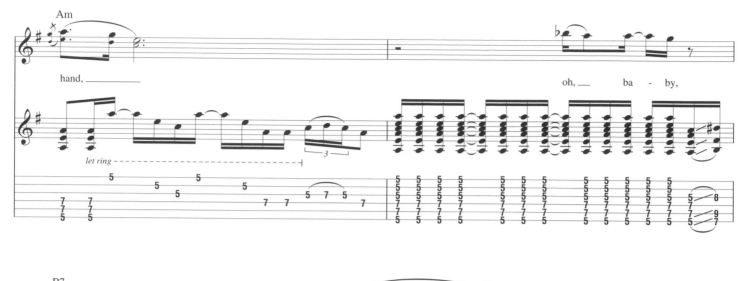

hand, _____ oh, __ ba - by,

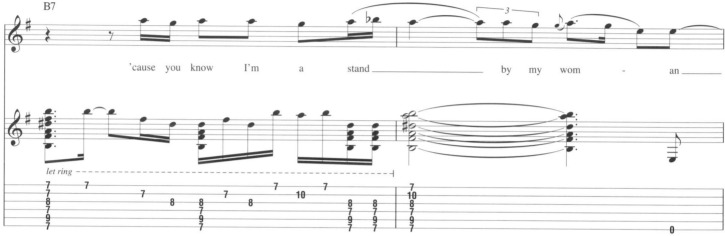

'cause you know I'm a stand _____ by my wom - an _____

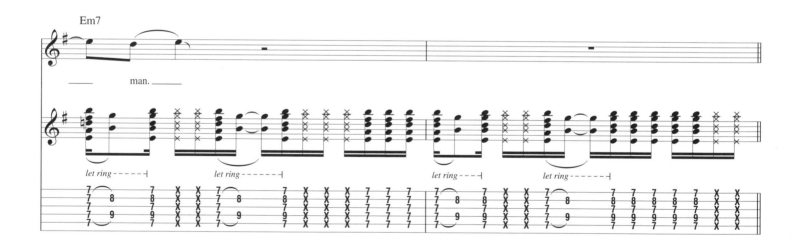

_____ man. _____

Chorus

Di - me mi a - mor, di - me mi a - mor que __ me

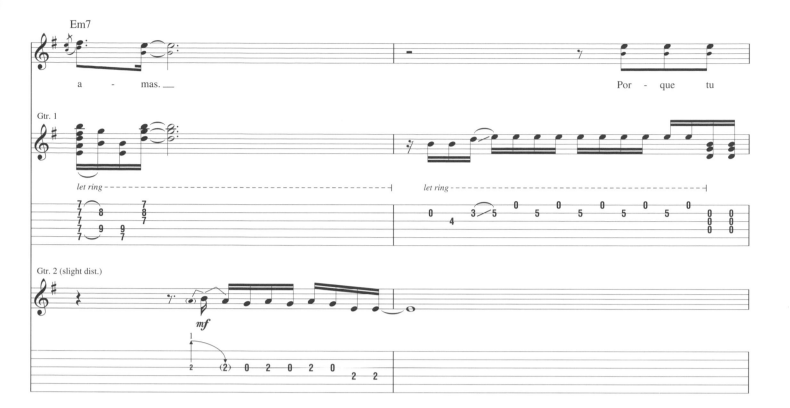

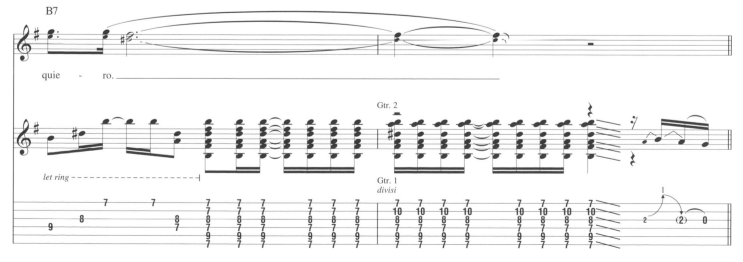

Guitar Solo

Gtr. 1 tacet

*Chord symbols reflect overall harmony.

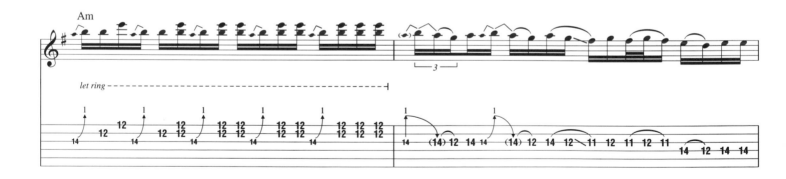

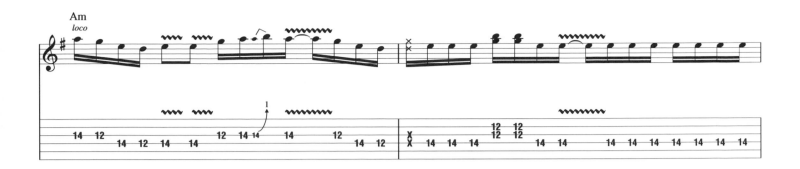

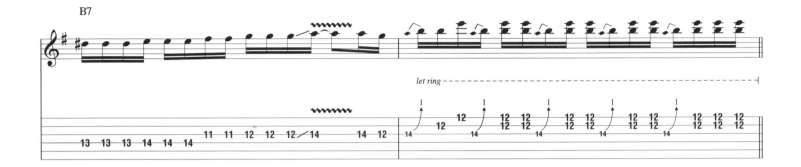

Chorus

Gtr. 1: w/ Rhy. Fig. 1   Gtr. 2: tacet

Di - me — mi a - mor,   di - me — mi a - mor que   me   a - mas.

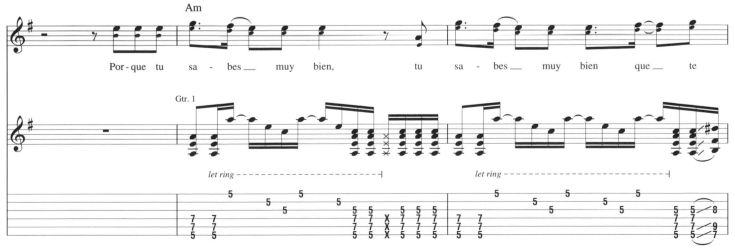

Por - que tu sa - bes — muy bien,   tu sa - bes — muy bien que   te

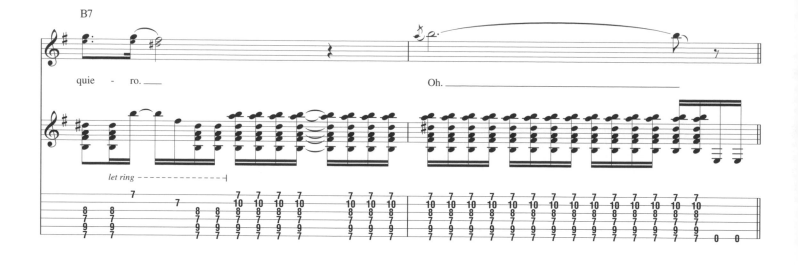

quie - ro. _____ Oh. _____

Interlude

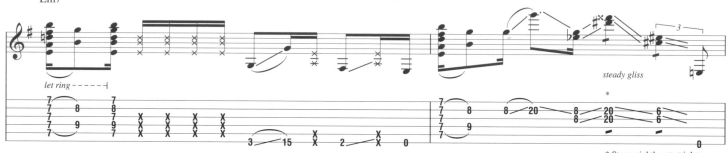

* Strum eighth-note triplets while sliding down strings.

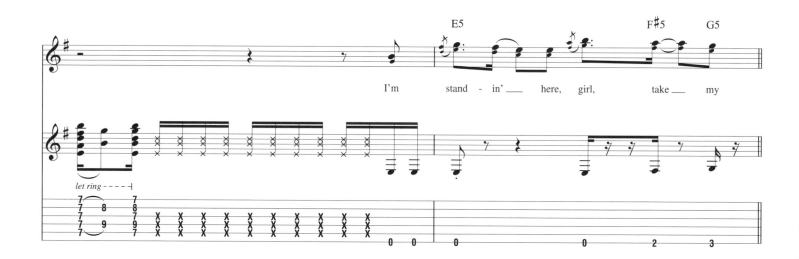

I'm stand - in' ___ here, girl, take ___ my

Chorus

hand, _____ oo, ___ ba - by,

40

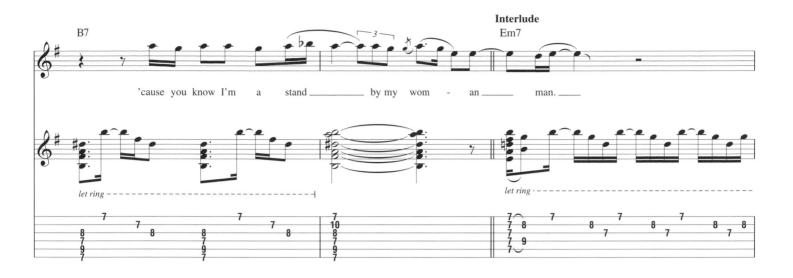

'cause you know I'm a stand _____ by my wom - an _____ man.

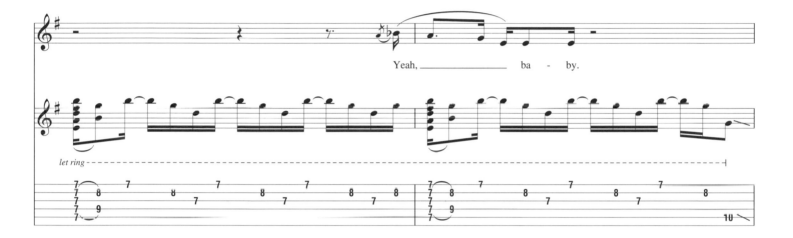

Yeah, _____ ba - by.

Outro-Guitar Solo

Gtr. 1 tacet

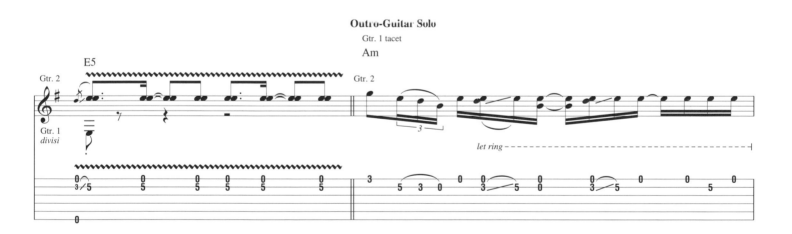

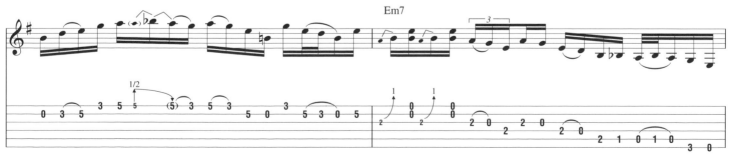

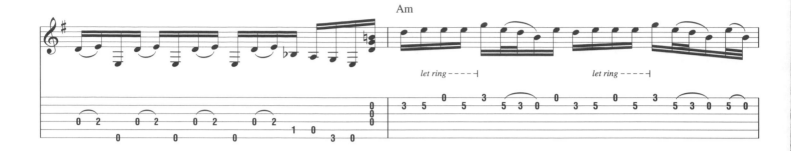

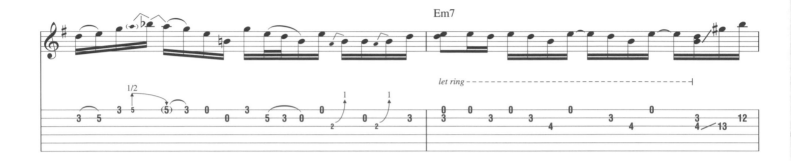

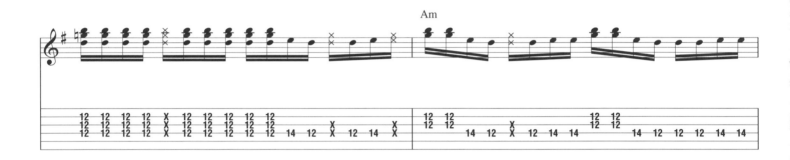

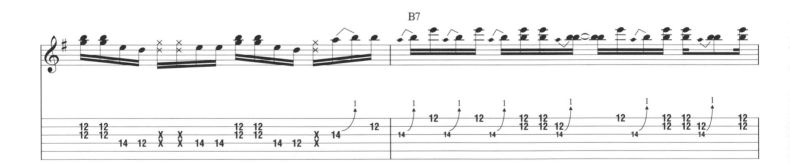

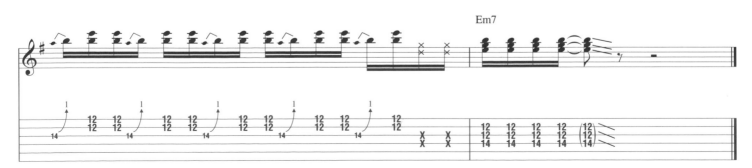

Hollywood

Words and Music by Henry Garza, Joey Garza and Ringo Garza

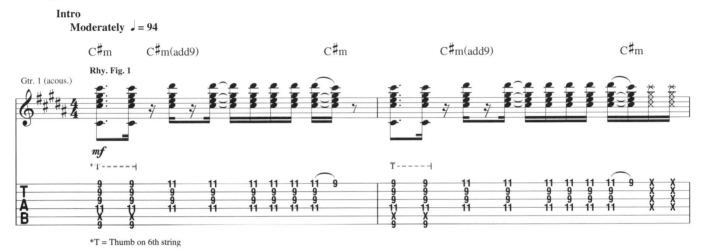

Tune down 1/2 step:
(low to high) E♭-A♭-D♭-G♭-B♭-E♭

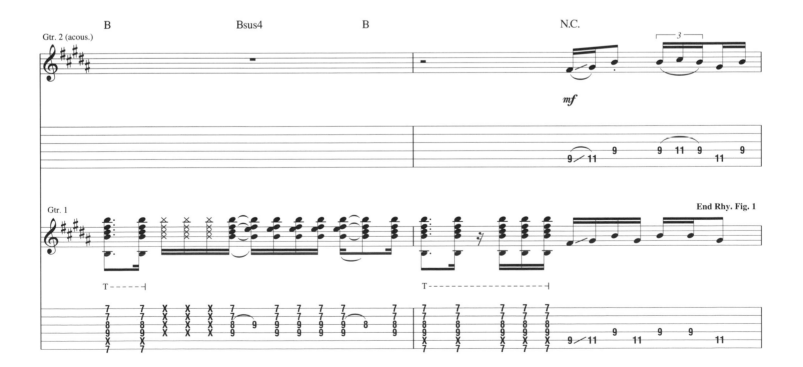

*T = Thumb on 6th string

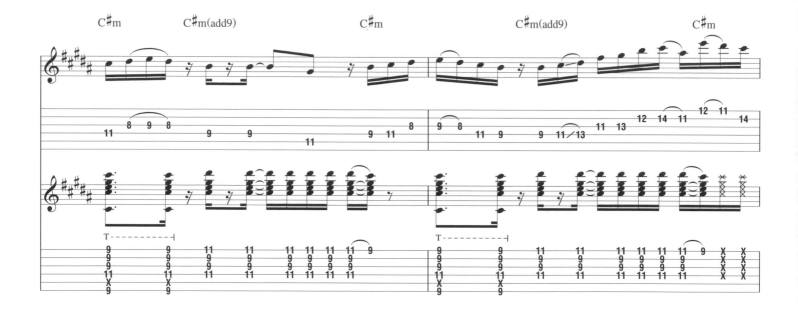

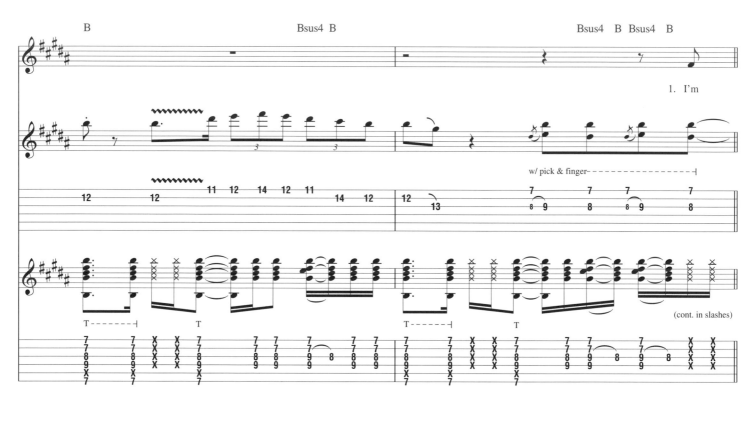

call - ing up my Cher - i to tell her that I'm gon - na leave,

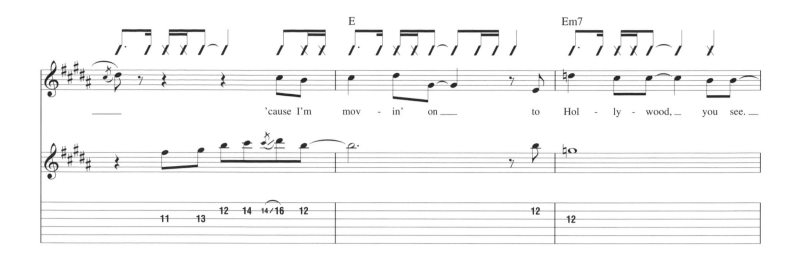

'cause I'm mov - in' on ____ to Hol - ly - wood, ____ you see.

Gtr. 1: w/ Rhy. Fig. 2

End Rhy. Fig. 2

It's al - ways been a life long ____ dream ____

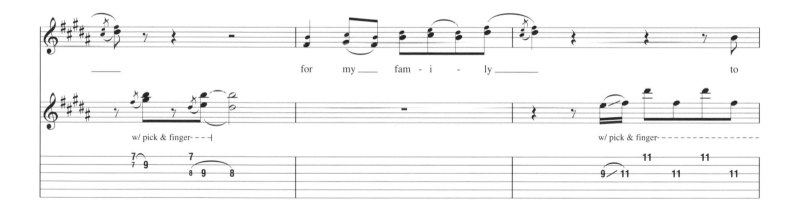

for my ____ fam - i - ly ____ to

w/ pick & finger- - - -⌐

w/ pick & finger- - - - - - - - - - - - - - - -

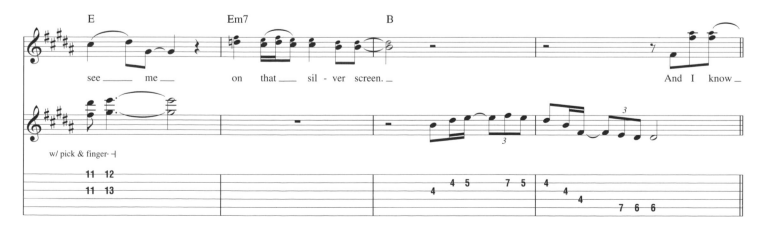

see ____ me ____ on that ____ sil - ver screen. ____ And I know ____

w/ pick & finger- -⌐

Chorus

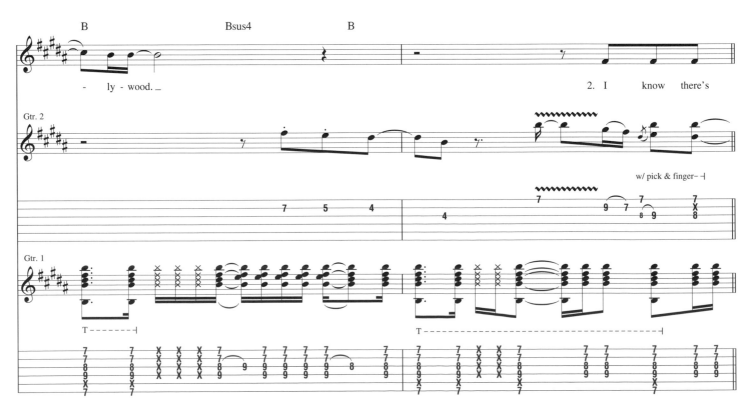

Verse

Gtr. 1: w/ Rhy. Fig. 2

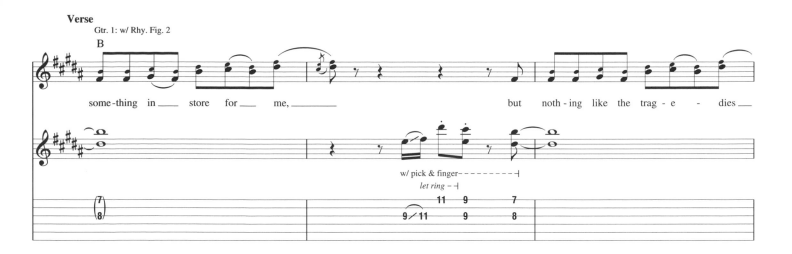

some-thing in ___ store for ___ me, ___ but noth-ing like the trag-e - dies ___

w/ pick & finger---------|
let ring -|

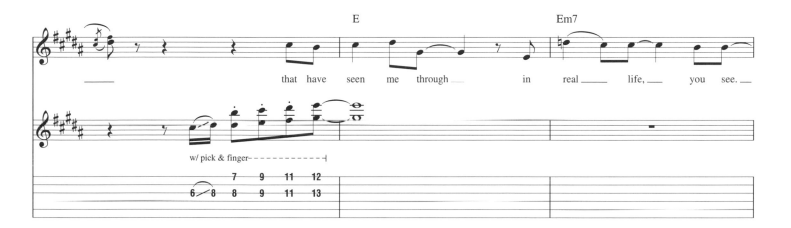

that have seen me through ___ in real ___ life, ___ you see. ___

w/ pick & finger-----------|

Chorus

Gtr. 1: w/ Rhy. Fig. 3 (3 times)

And I know ___ I can't ___ go wrong ___

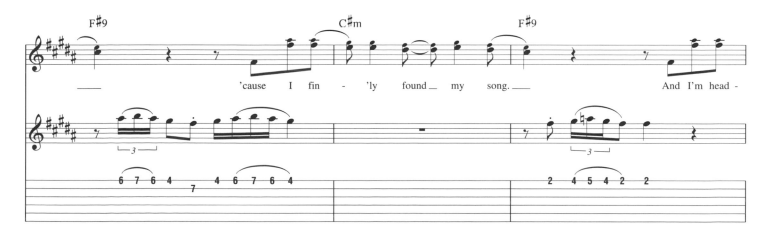

___ 'cause I fin - 'ly found ___ my song. ___ And I'm head -

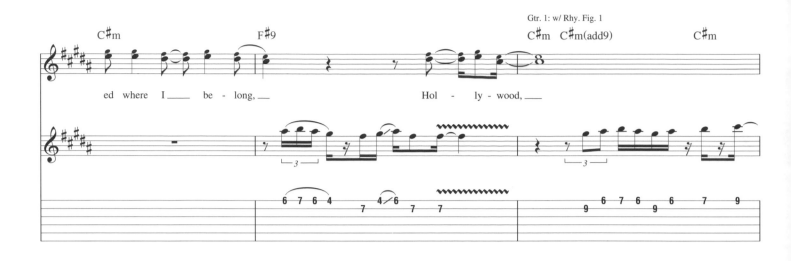

ed where I___ be - long,___ Hol - ly - wood,___

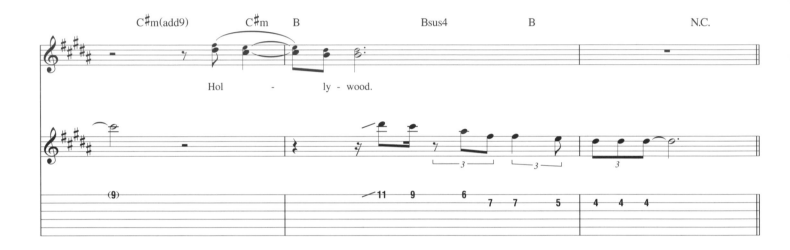

Hol - ly - wood.

Guitar Solo

Gtr. 1: w/ Rhy. Fig. 1 (1 3/4 times)

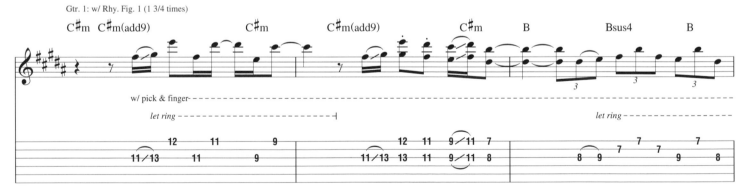

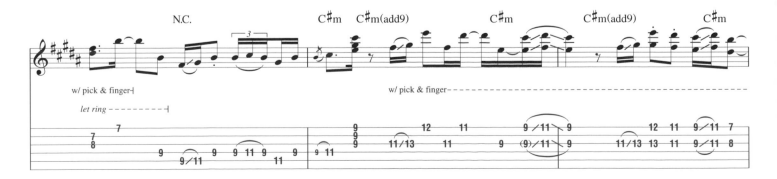

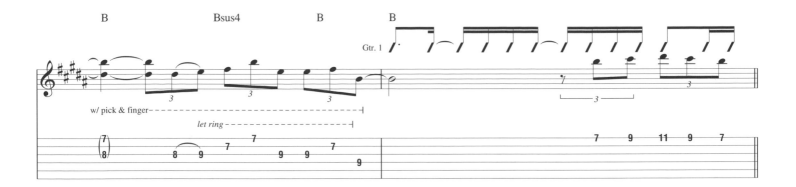

Bridge

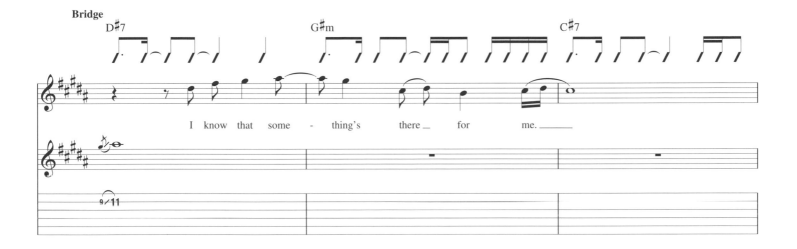

I know that some - thing's there __ for me. __

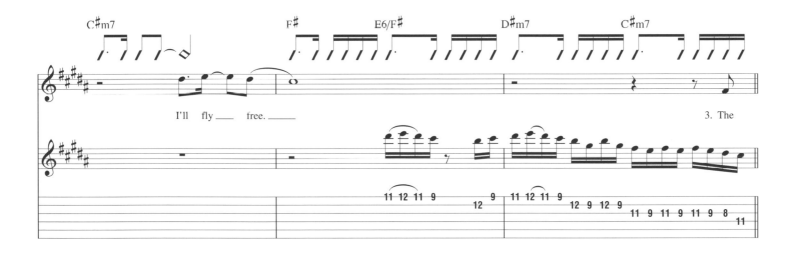

I'll fly __ free. __

3. The

Verse

Gtr. 1: w/ Rhy. Fig. 2

next time that __ you see __ me __ I'll be done with mis - er - y. __ I'll be

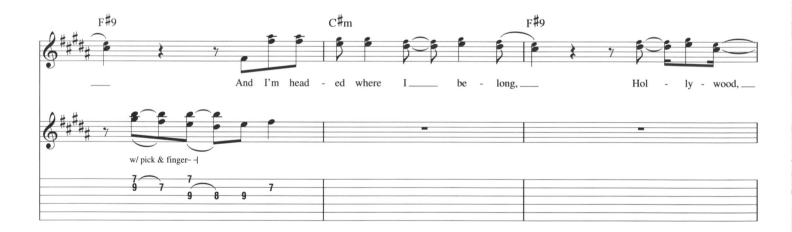

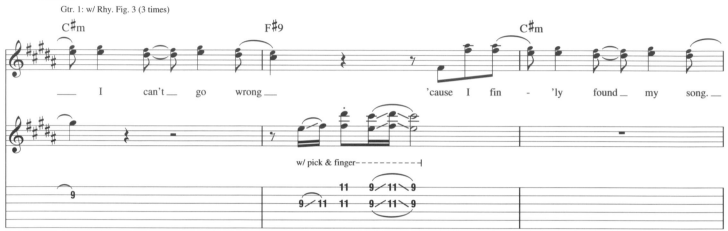

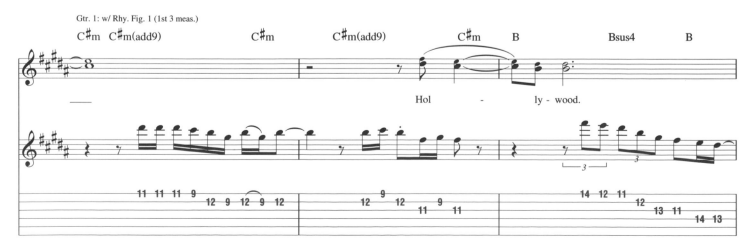

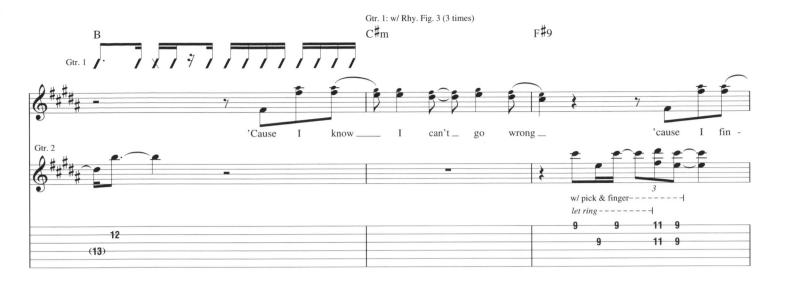

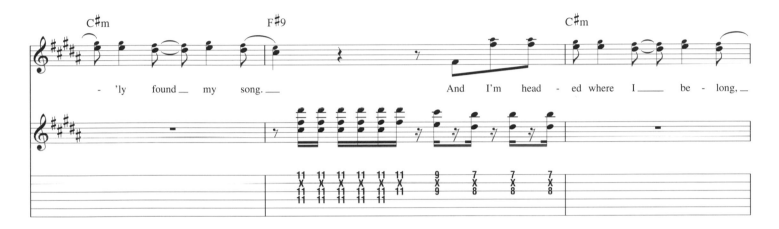

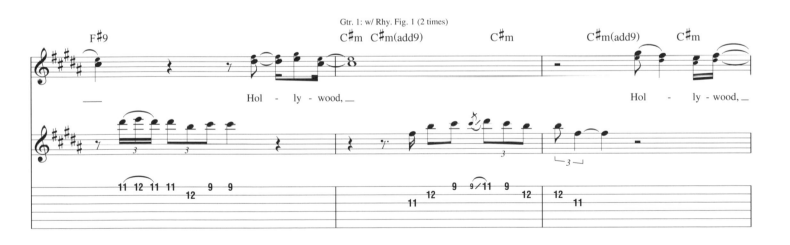

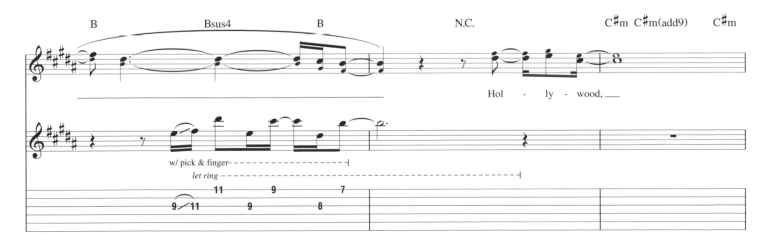

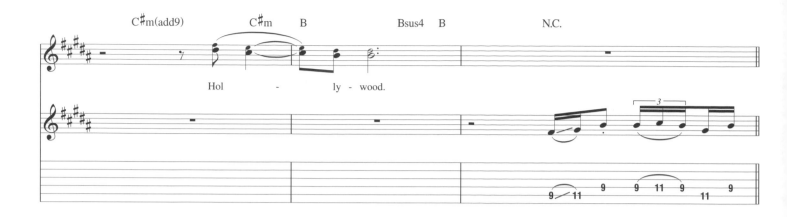

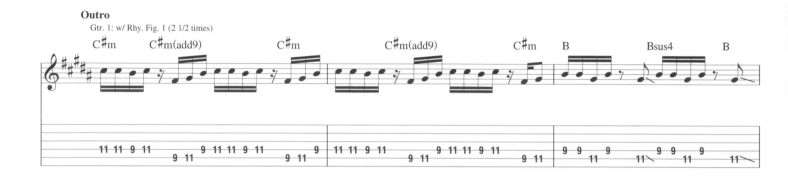

Outro

Gtr. 1: w/ Rhy. Fig. 1 (2 1/2 times)

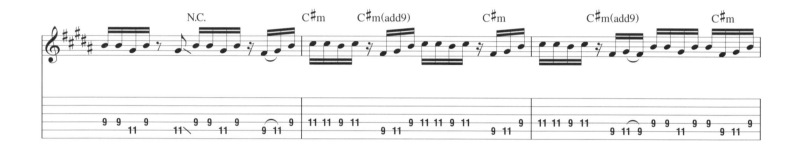

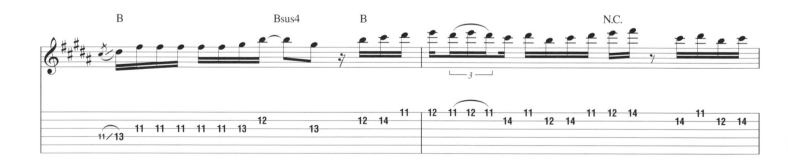

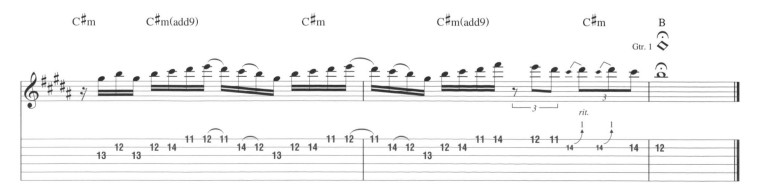

More Than Love

Words and Music by Henry Garza, Joey Garza and Ringo Garza

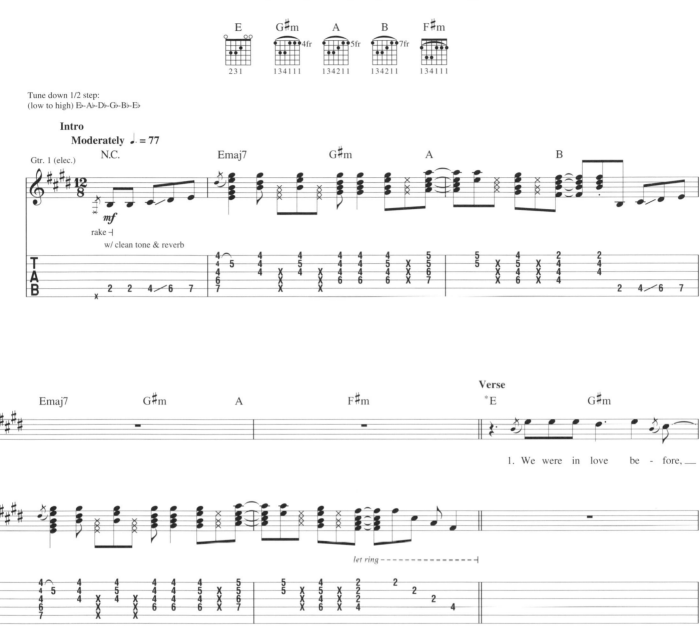

Tune down 1/2 step:
(low to high) Eb-Ab-Db-Gb-Bb-Eb

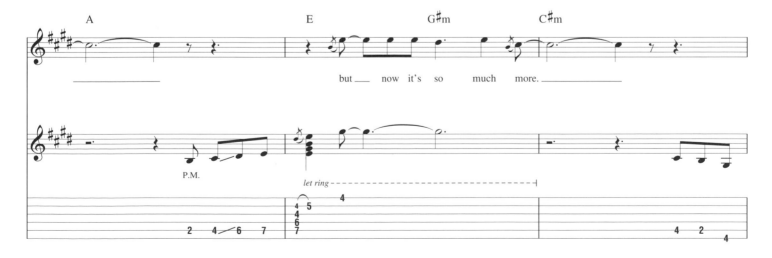

*Chord symbols reflect overall harmony.

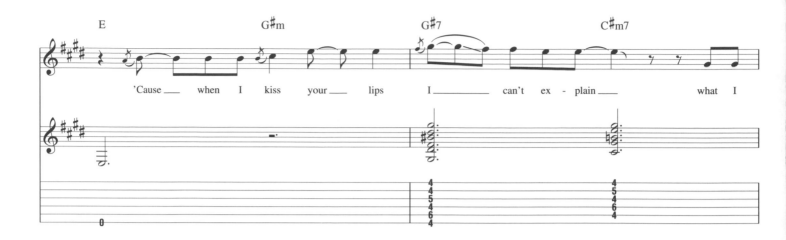

'Cause __ when I kiss your __ lips I __ can't ex - plain __ what I

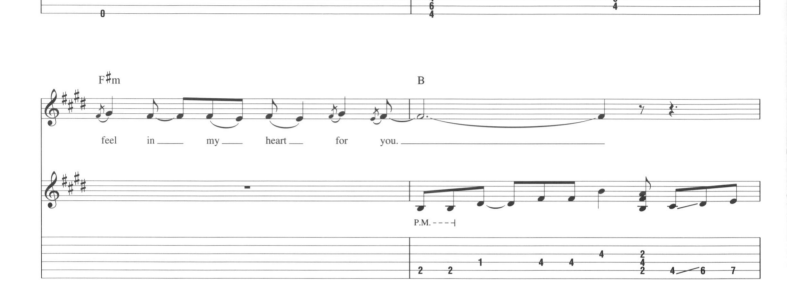

feel in __ my __ heart __ for you. __

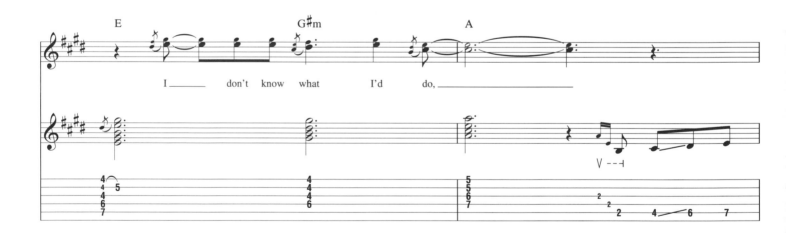

I __ don't know what I'd do, __

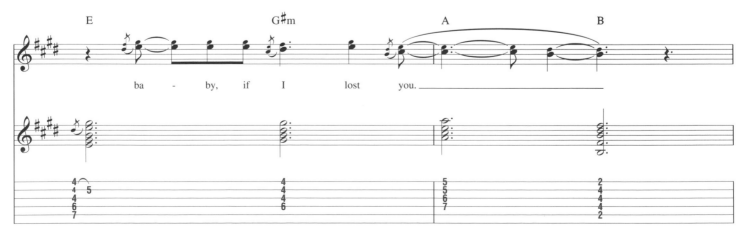

ba - by, if I lost you. __

'Cause I've been with-out you ___ and I ___ know how it feels, ___ and I

can't be ___ a - lone ___ an - y - more. ___

Chorus

I know ___ it's more than love, ___ ba - by, ___ I can feel ___ it

*Doubled throughout

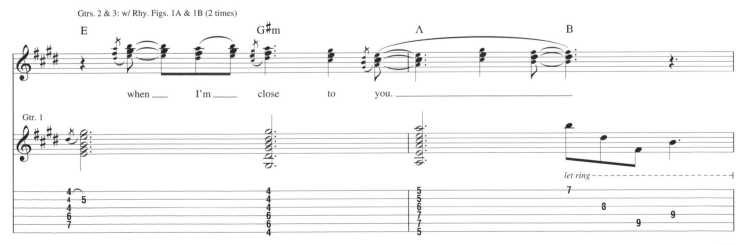

when ___ I'm ___ close to you.

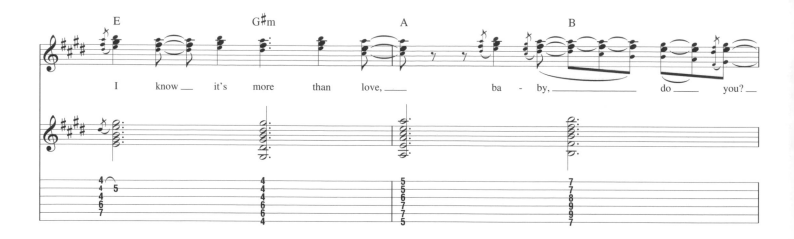

I know ___ it's more than love, ___ ba - by, ___ do ___ you?

Bridge

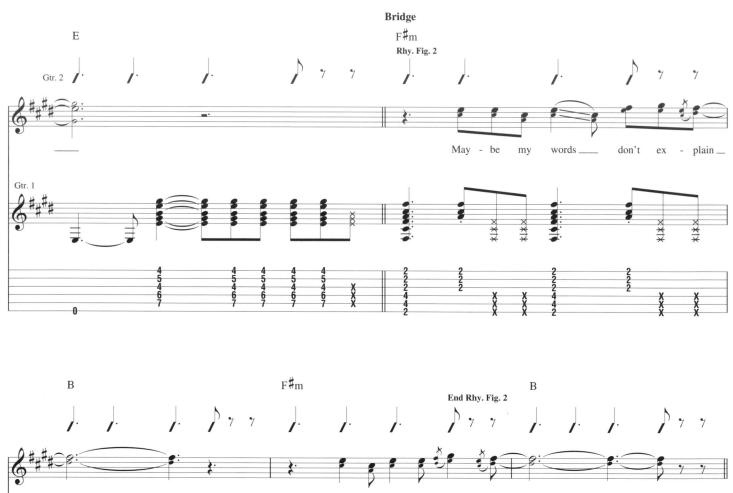

May - be my words ___ don't ex - plain ___

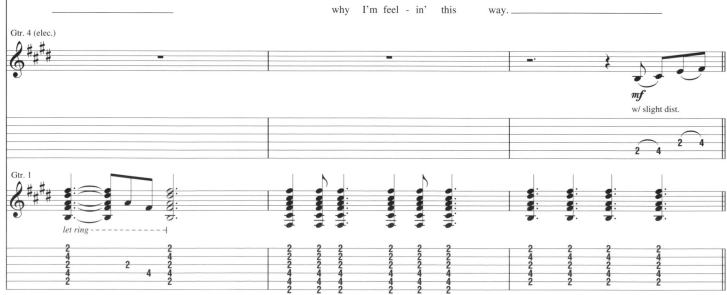

why I'm feel - in' this way. ___

Guitar Solo

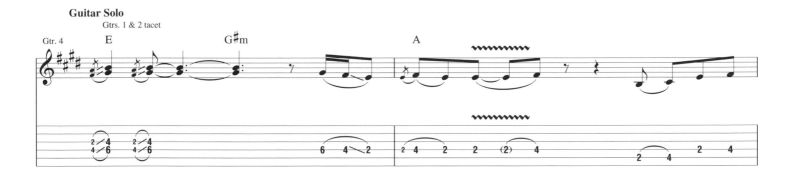

Bridge

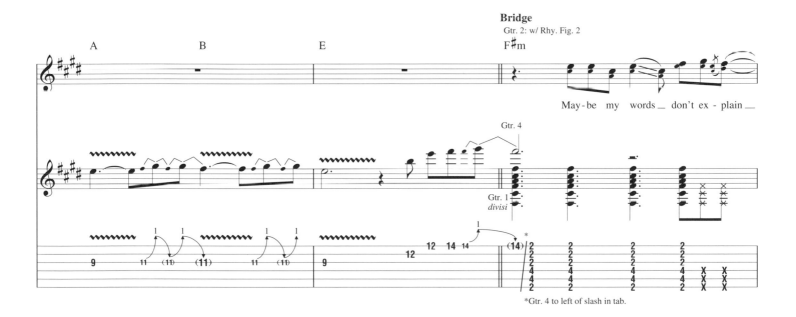

May-be my words __ don't ex - plain __

*Gtr. 4 to left of slash in tab.

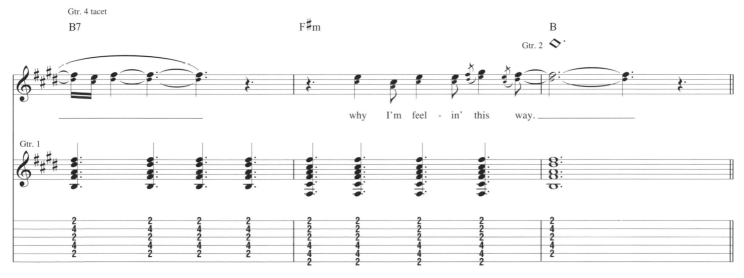

why I'm feel - in' this way. __

Verse

Gtrs. 1 & 2 tacet

2. I _____ don't know what I'd do, _____

ba - by, if I lost you. _____

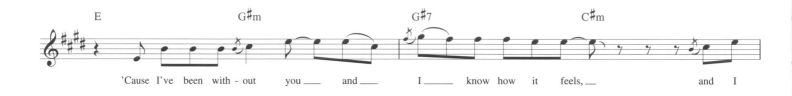

'Cause I've been with-out you _____ and _____ I _____ know how it feels, _____ and I

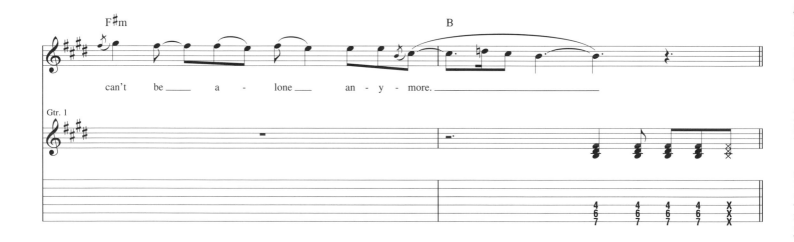

can't be _____ a - lone _____ an - y - more. _____

Outro-Chorus

Gtr. 1: w/ Rhy. Fig. 1 (3 times)
Gtr. 2: w/ Rhy. Fig. 1A (5 times)

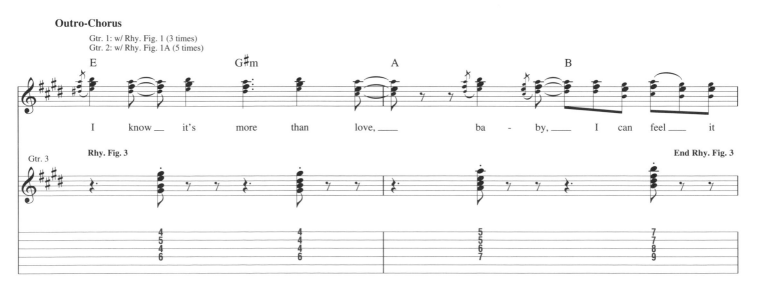

I know _____ it's more than love, _____ ba - by, _____ I can feel _____ it

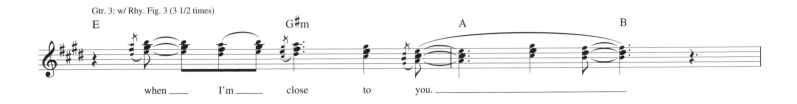

when ____ I'm ____ close to you. ____

I know ____ it's more than love, ____ ba - by, ____ I can feel ____ it

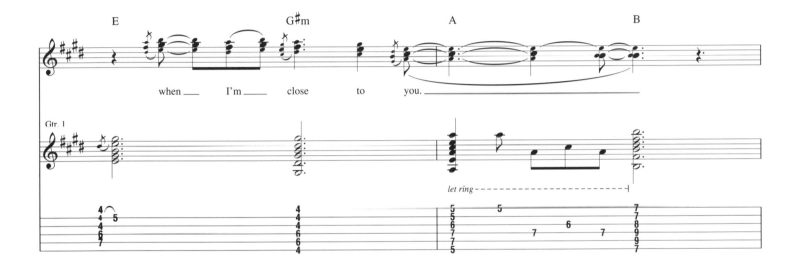

when ____ I'm ____ close to you. ____

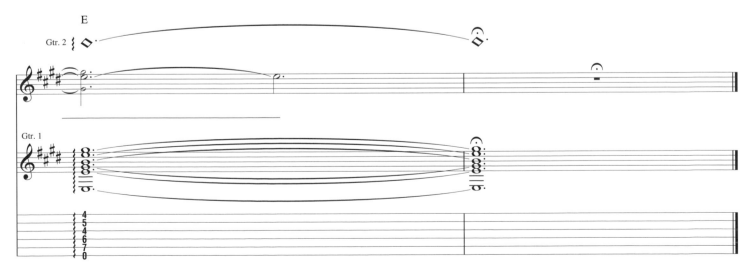

I know ____ it's more than love, ____ ba - by, ____ do ____ you? ____

Nobody Else

Words and Music by Henry Garza, Joey Garza, Ringo Garza and Kevin Wommack

Tune down 1/2 step:
(low to high) E♭-A♭-D♭-G♭-B♭-E♭

Intro
Moderately slow ♩ = 82

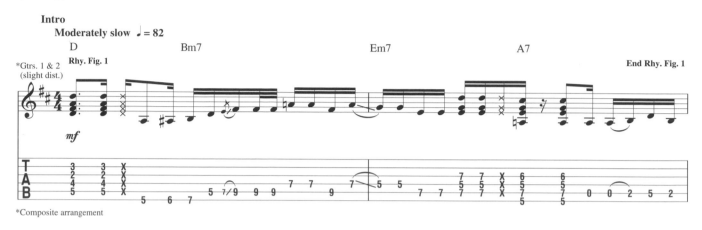

*Gtrs. 1 & 2
(slight dist.)

*Composite arrangement

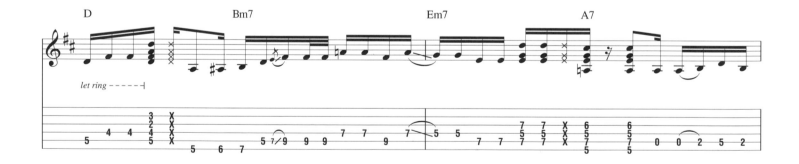

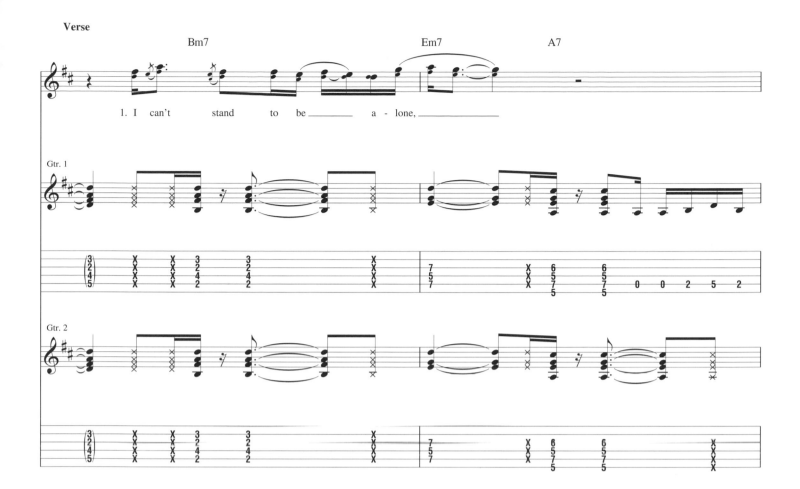

Verse

1. I can't stand to be _____ a - lone, _____

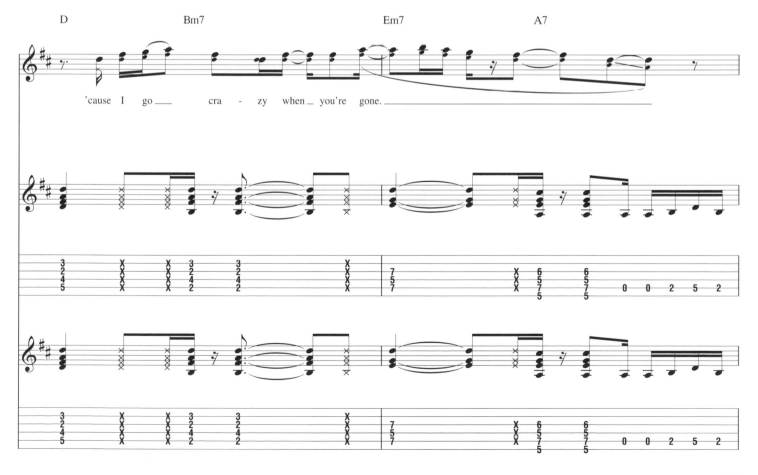

'cause I go _____ cra - zy when ___ you're gone. _____

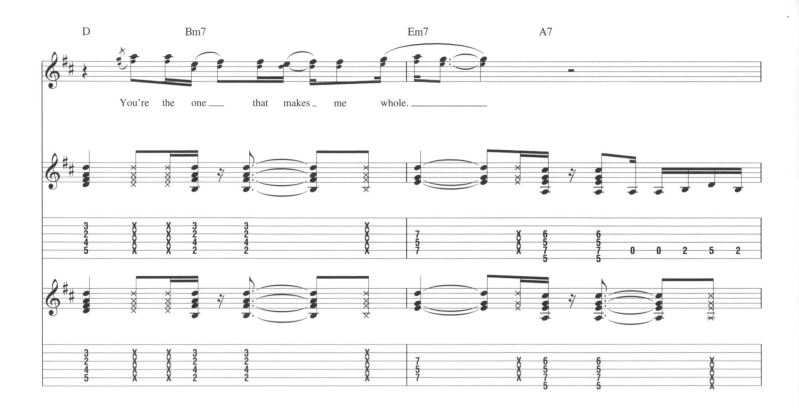

You're the one ___ that makes ___ me whole. _____

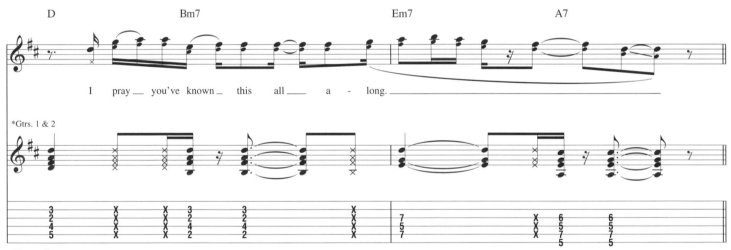

I pray ___ you've known ___ this all ___ a - long. _____

*Gtrs. 1 & 2

*Composite arrangement

Pre-Chorus

Ev -'ry-thing is gon-na be ___ al - right, ___ I wan-na be with you all of ___ my ___ life.

Interlude

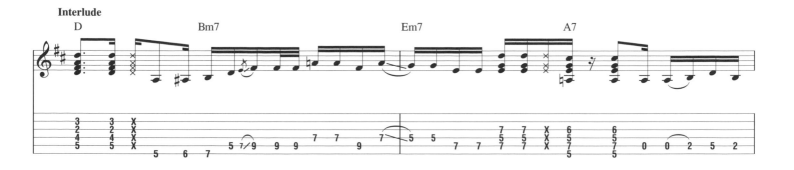

Verse

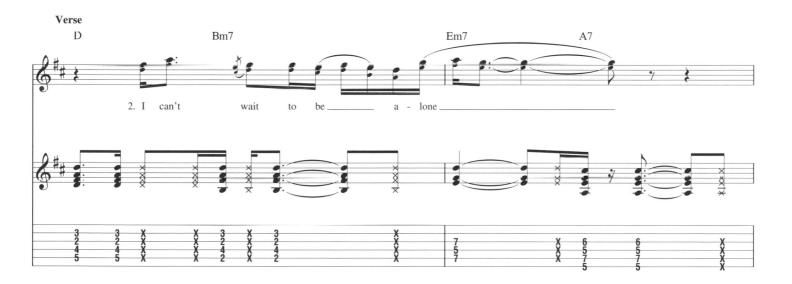

2. I can't wait to be _____ a - lone _____

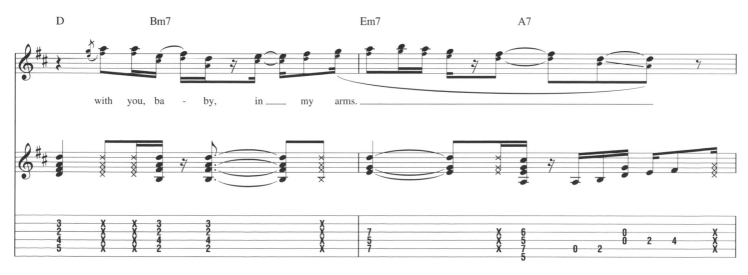

with you, ba - by, in ___ my arms. _____

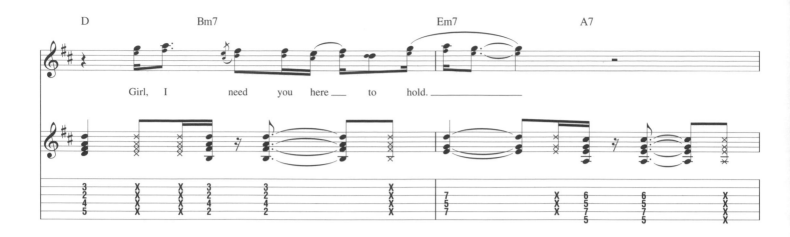

Girl, I need you here to hold.

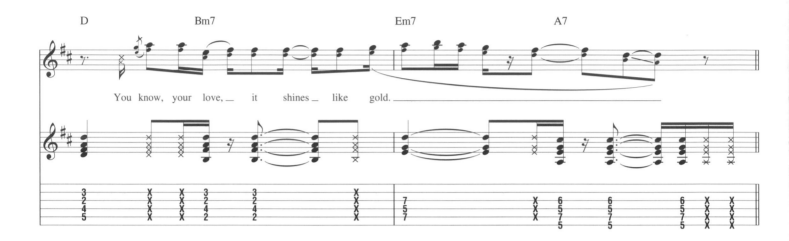

You know, your love, it shines like gold.

Pre-Chorus

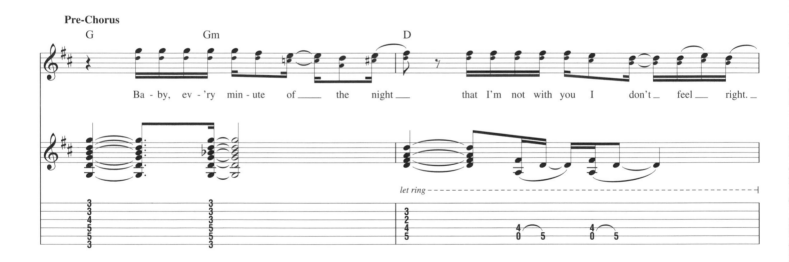

Baby, ev-'ry min-ute of the night that I'm not with you I don't feel right.

let ring

Chorus

Gtrs. 1 & 2: w/ Rhy. Fig. 1

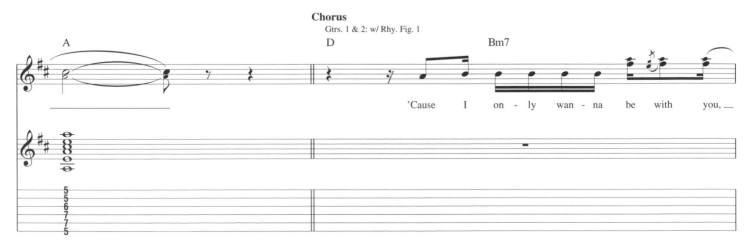

'Cause I on-ly wan-na be with you,

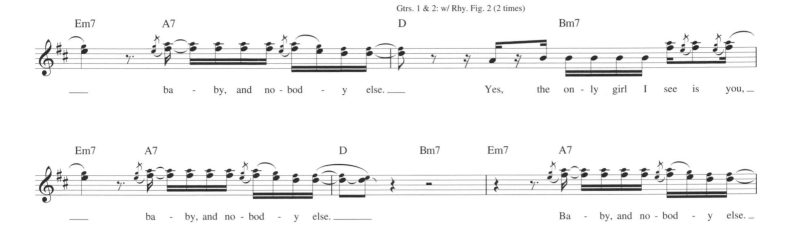

ba - by, and no - bod - y else. _____ Yes, the on - ly girl I see is you, _____

ba - by, and no - bod - y else. _____ Ba - by, and no - bod - y else. _____

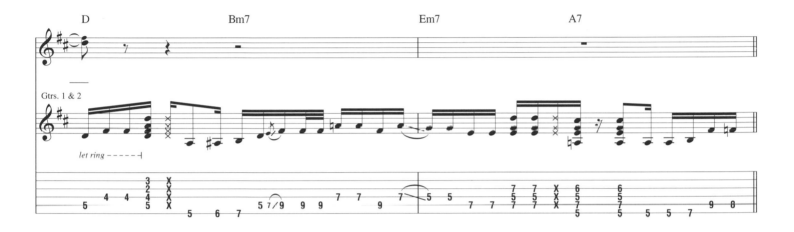

Guitar Solo

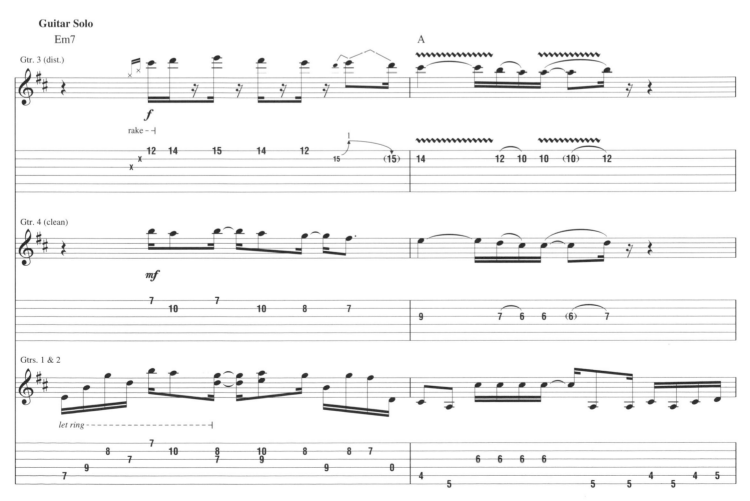

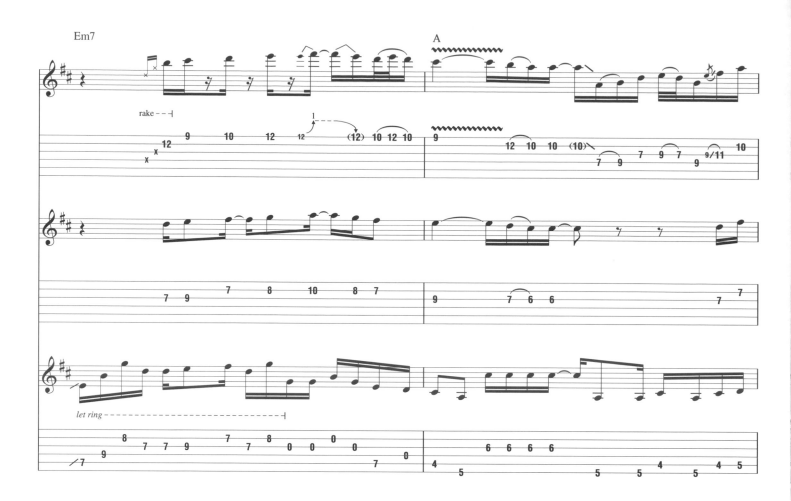

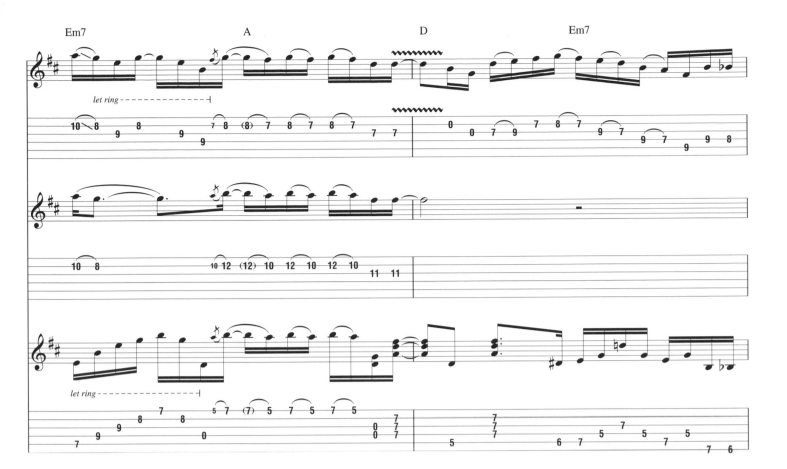

Verse

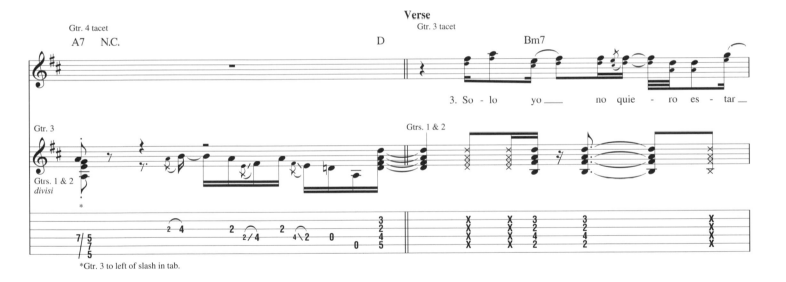

3. So - lo   yo___   no quie - ro es - tar___

*Gtr. 3 to left of slash in tab.

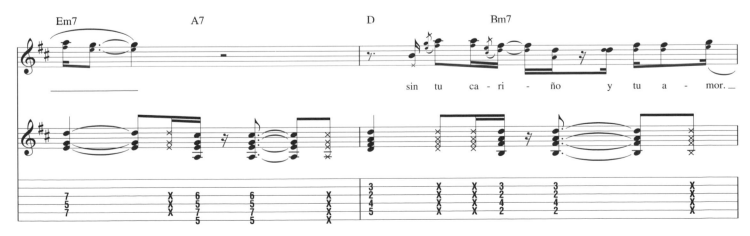

sin   tu   ca - ri - ño   y   tu   a - mor.

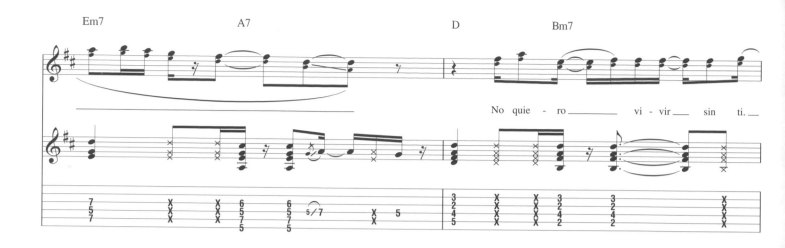

No quie - ro____ vi - vir__ sin ti.__

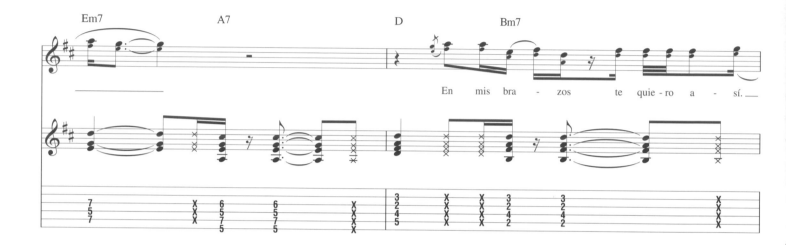

En mis bra - zos te quie - ro a - sí._

Pre-Chorus

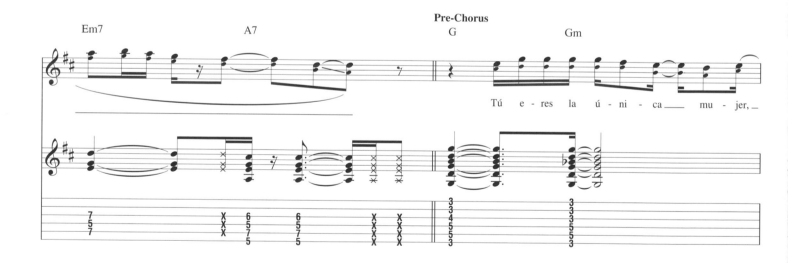

Tú e - res la ú - ni - ca__ mu - jer,__

__ te quie - ro en mi vi - da por tú__ que - rer.__

Chorus

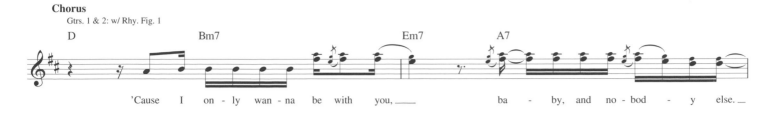

'Cause I on-ly wan-na be with you, ____ ba — by, and no-bod — y else. ____

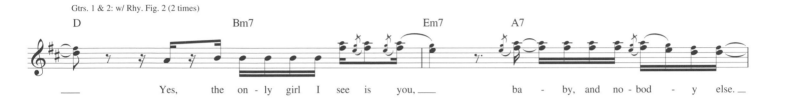

____ Yes, the on-ly girl I see is you, ____ ba — by, and no-bod — y else. ____

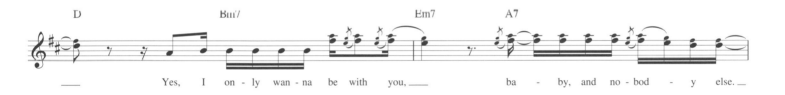

____ Yes, I on-ly wan-na be with you, ____ ba — by, and no-bod — y else. ____

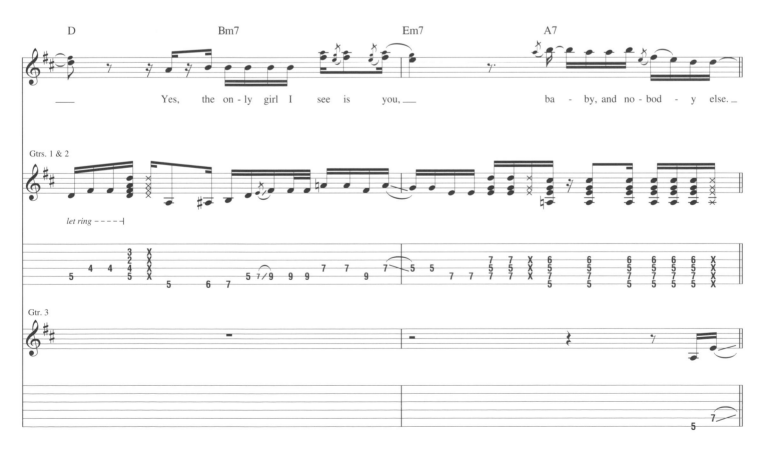

____ Yes, the on-ly girl I see is you, ____ ba — by, and no-bod — y else. ____

Outro-Guitar Solo

Gtrs. 1 & 2: w/ Rhy. Fig. 1

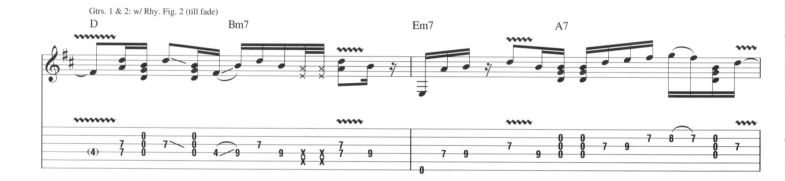

Gtrs. 1 & 2: w/ Rhy. Fig. 2 (till fade)

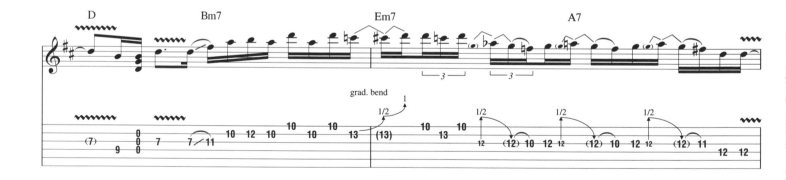

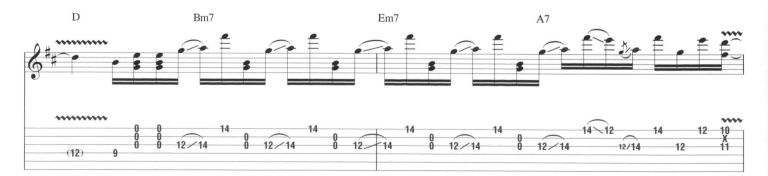

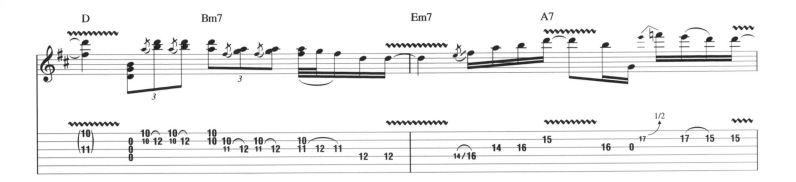

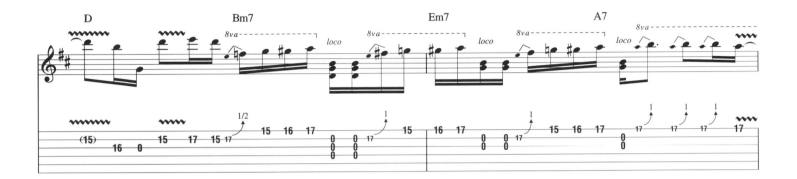

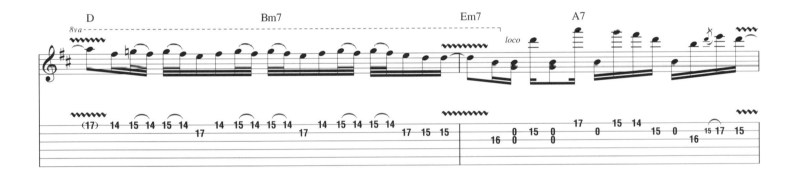

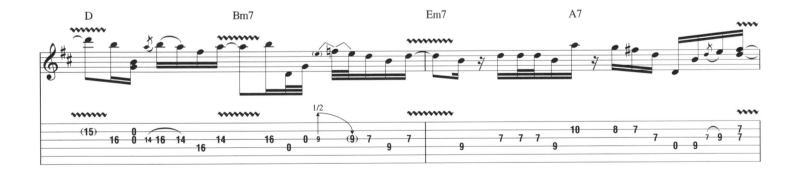

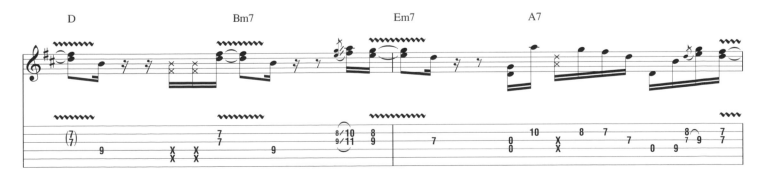

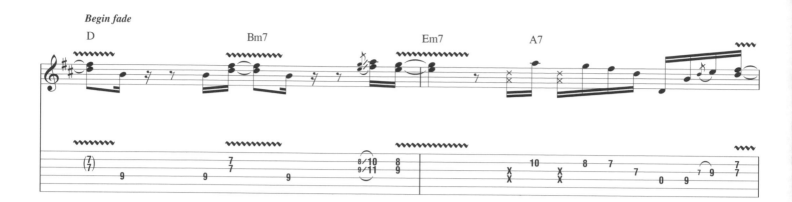

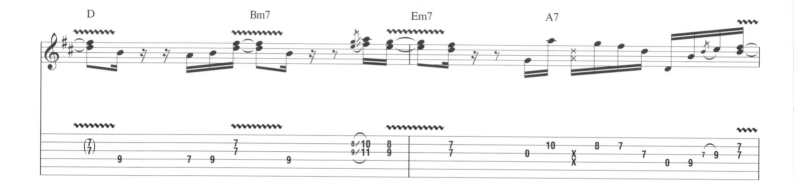

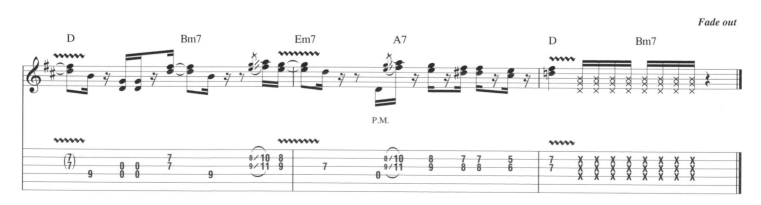

Onda

Words and Music by Henry Garza, Joey Garza and Ringo Garza

Tune down 1/2 step:
(low to high) Eb-Ab-Db-Gb-Bb-Eb

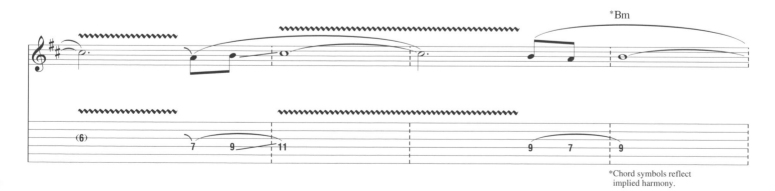

*Chord symbols reflect
implied harmony.

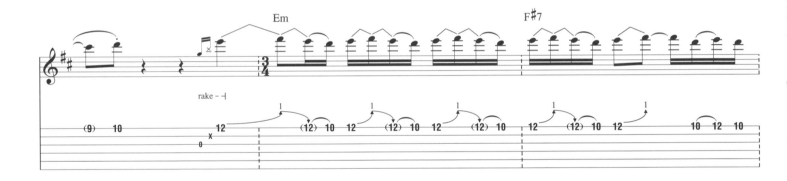

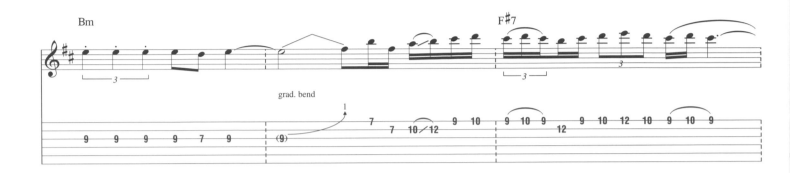

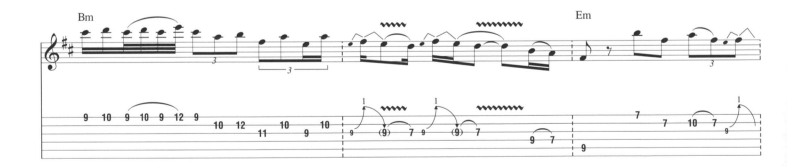

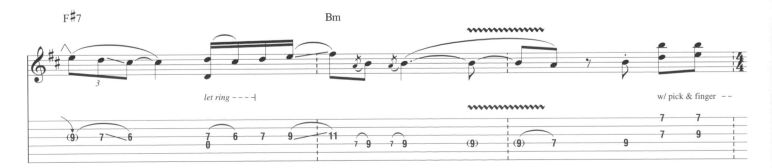

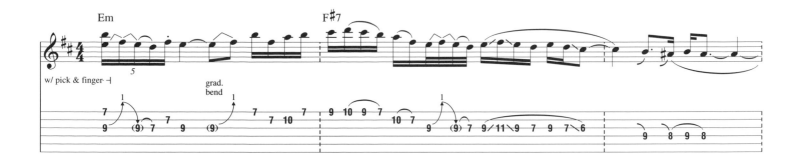

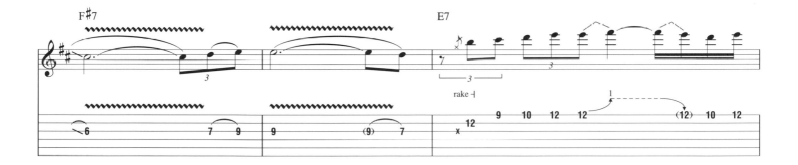

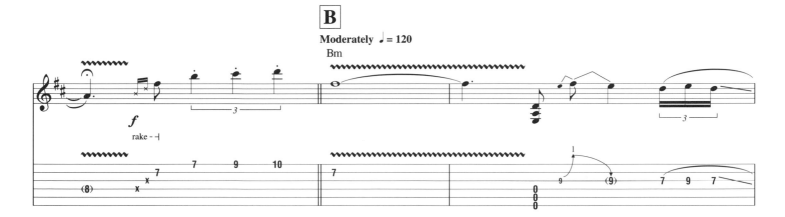

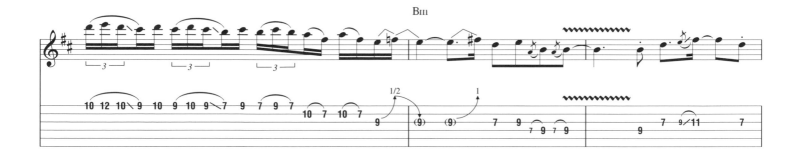

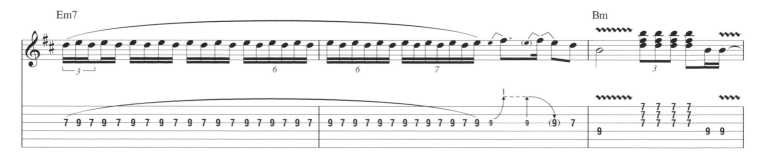

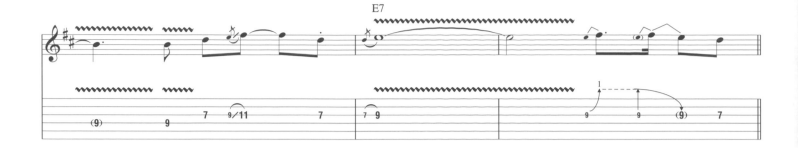

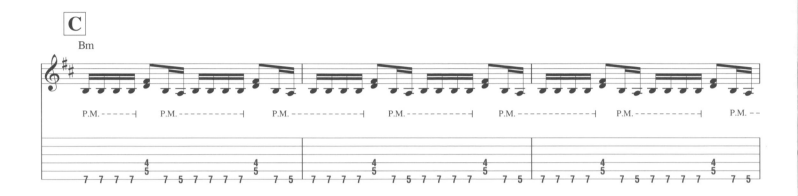

C

D

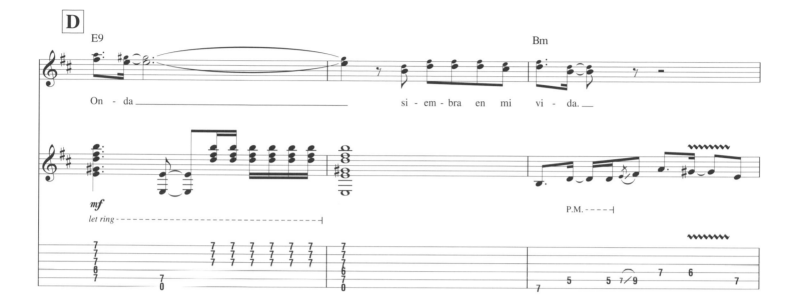

On - da _____ si - em - bra en mi vi - da. _____

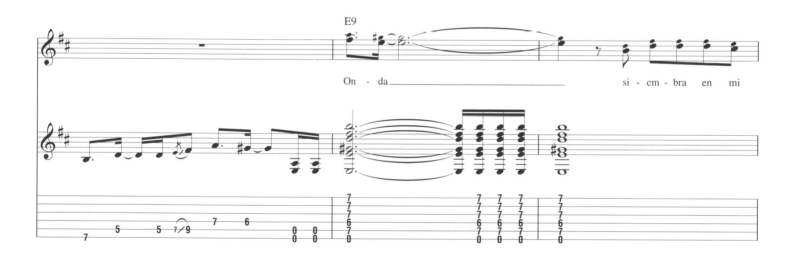

On - da _____ si - em - bra en mi

Bm _____ vi - da. _____ E9 _____ On - da _____

si - em - bra en mi vi - da.

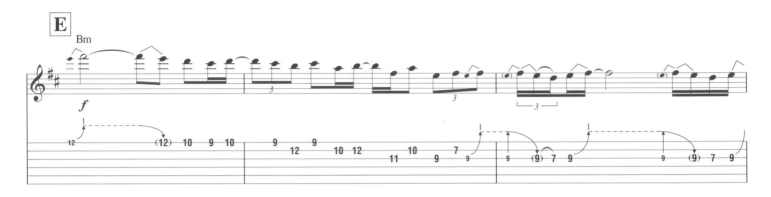

E Bm

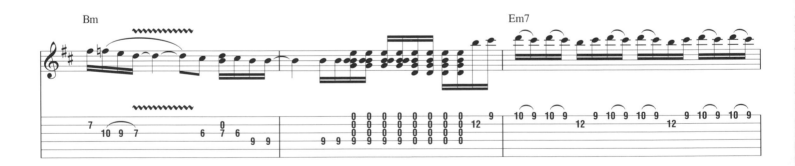

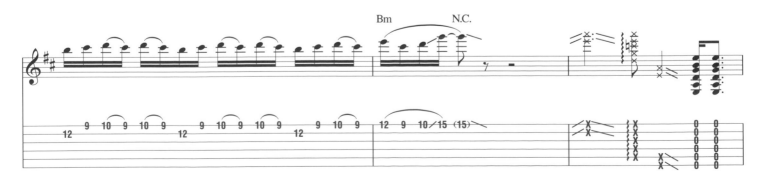

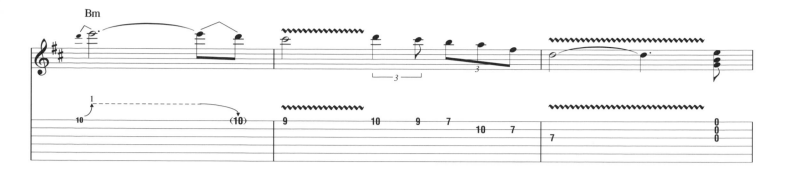

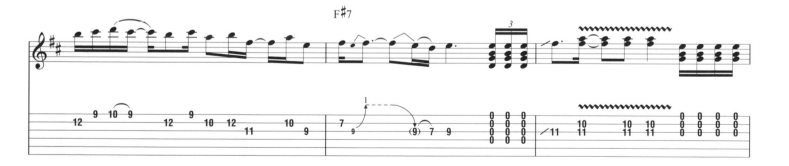

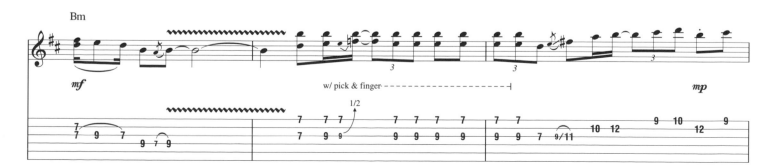

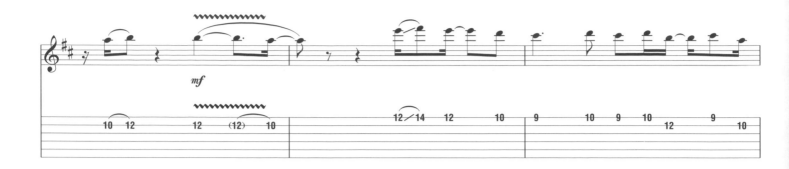

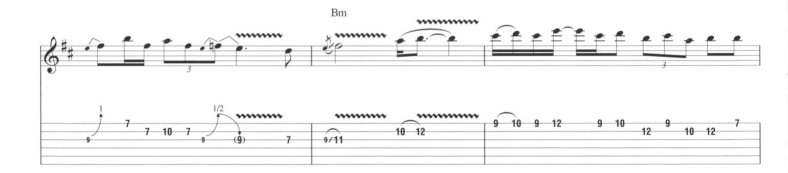

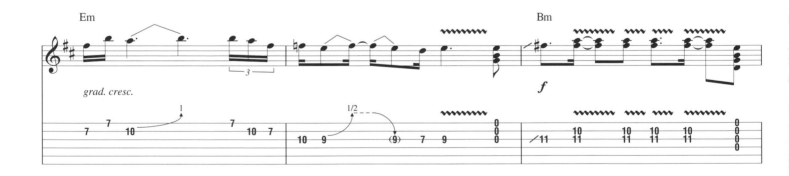

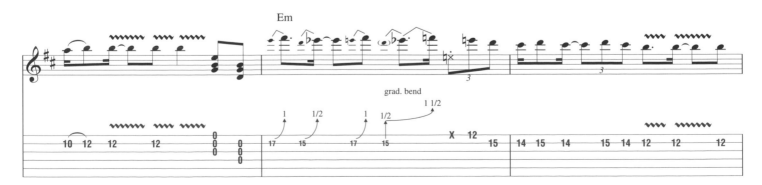

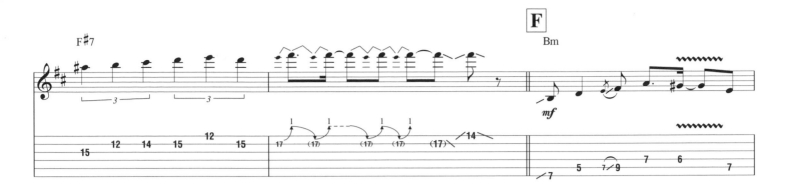

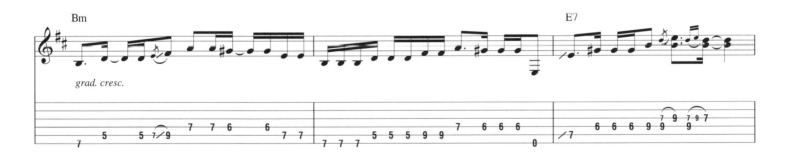

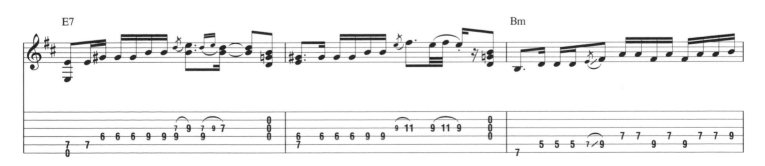

G

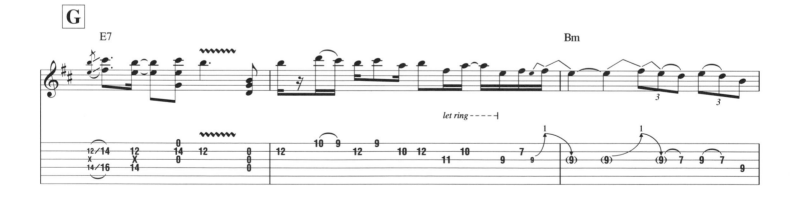

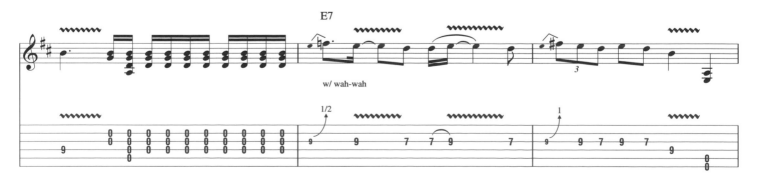

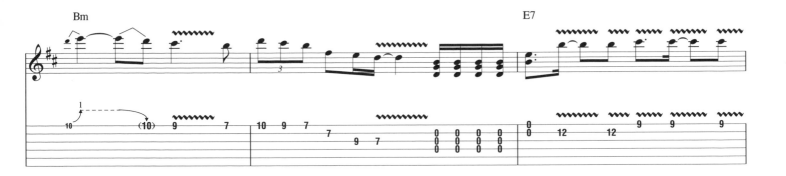

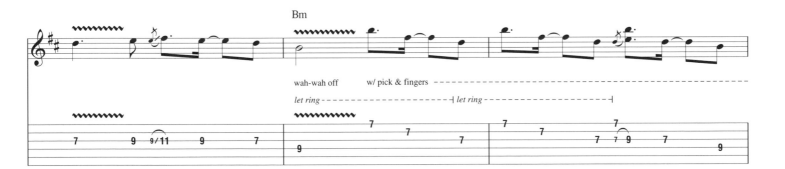

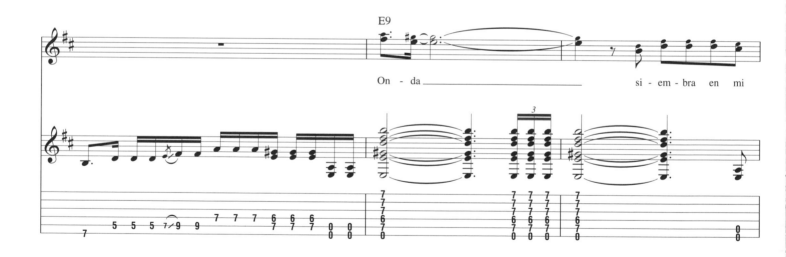

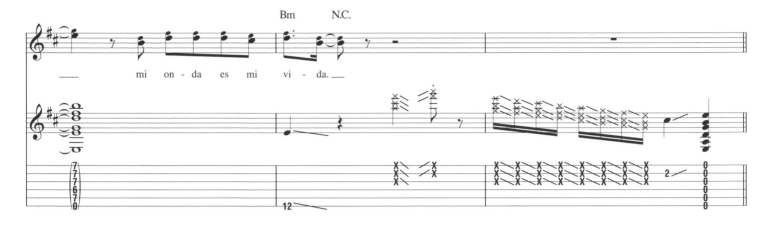

mi on - da es mi vi - da. ___

I

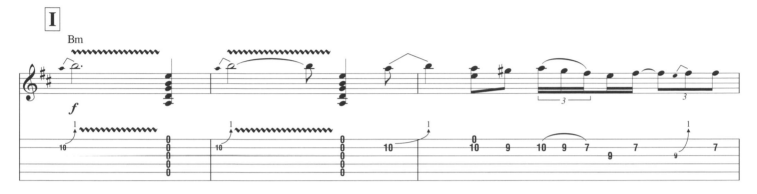

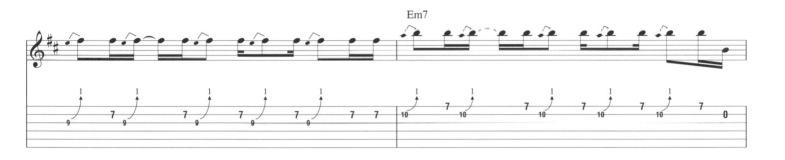

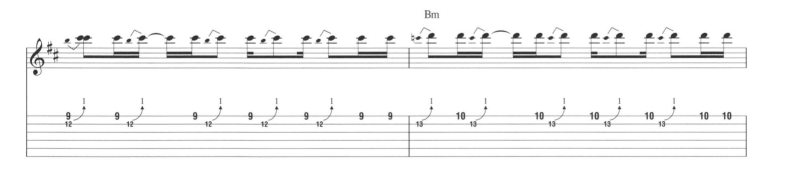

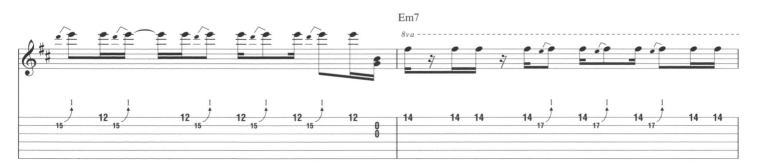

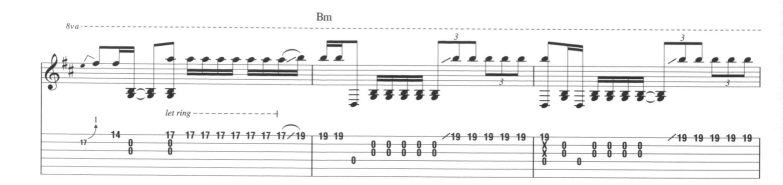

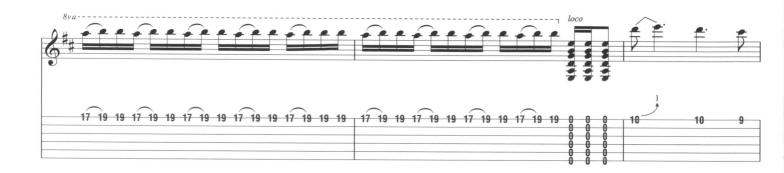

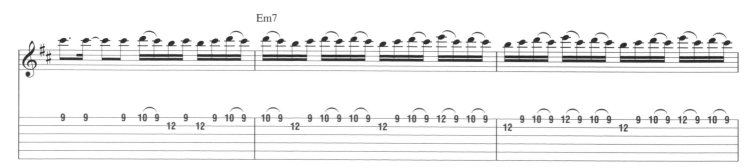

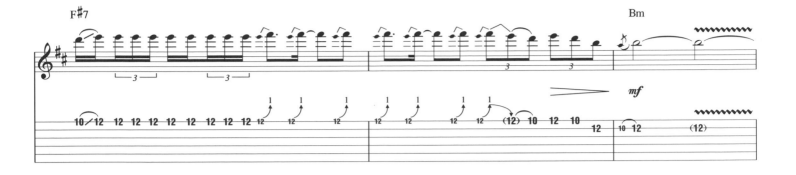

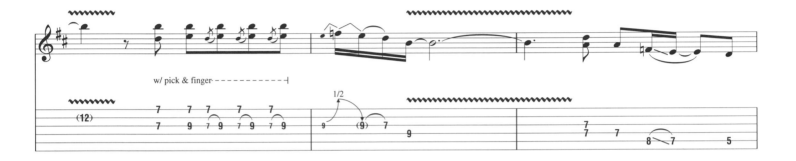

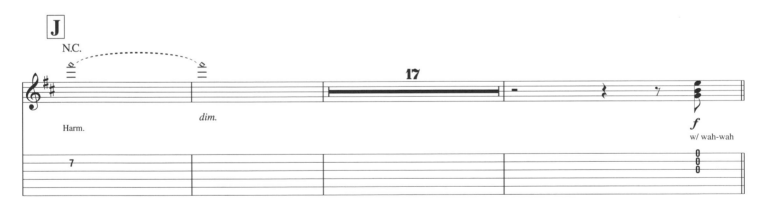

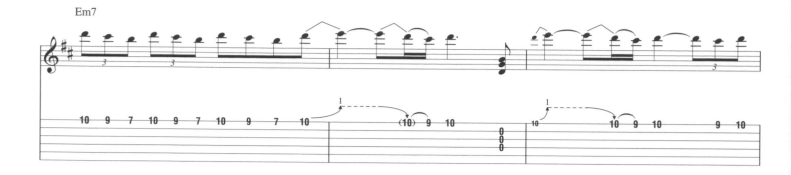

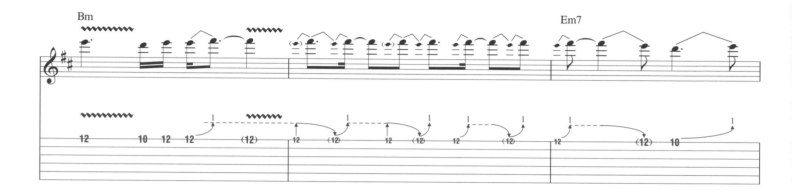

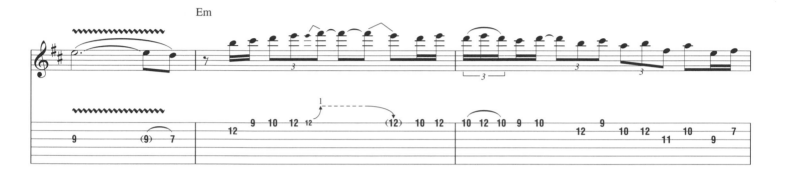

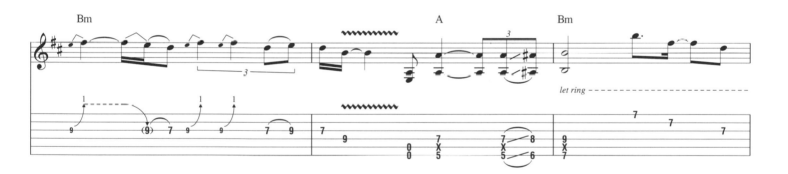

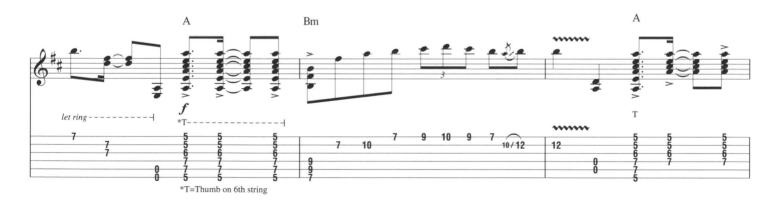

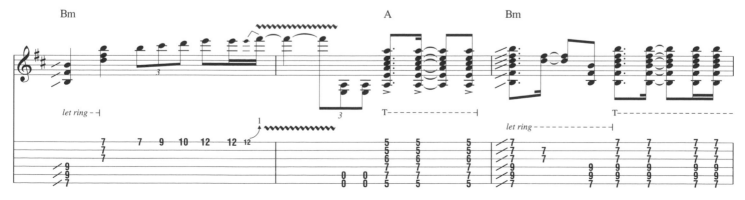

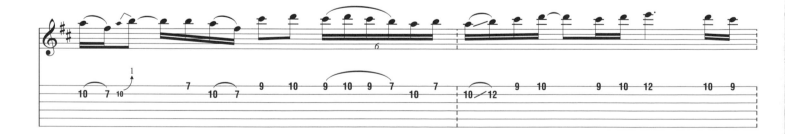

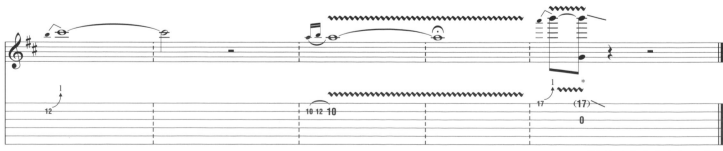

*G string is inadvertently bumped.

Real Emotions

Words and Music by Henry Garza, Joey Garza, Ringo Garza and Kevin Wommack

Tune down 1/2 step:
(low to high) Eb-Ab-Db-Gb-Bb-Eb

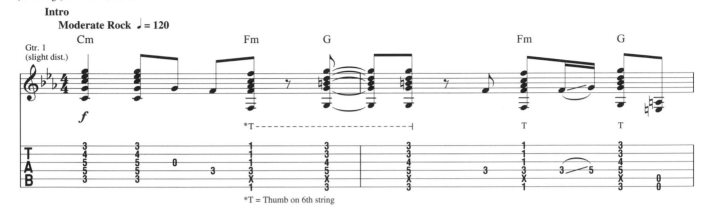

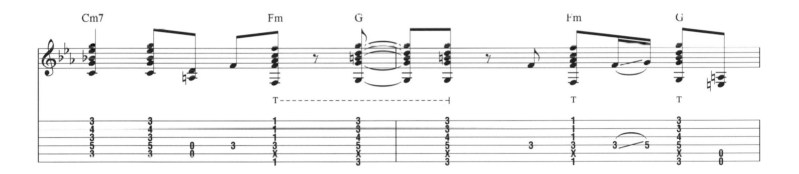

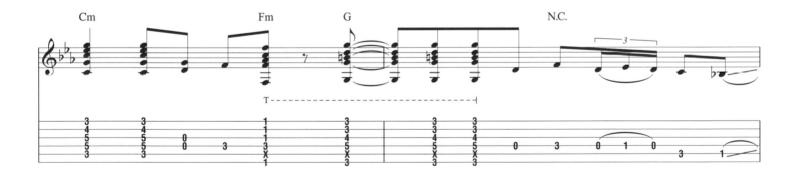

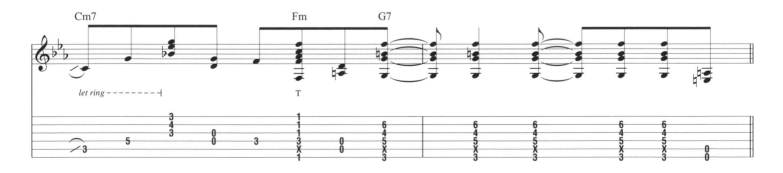

*Chord symbols reflect overall harmony.

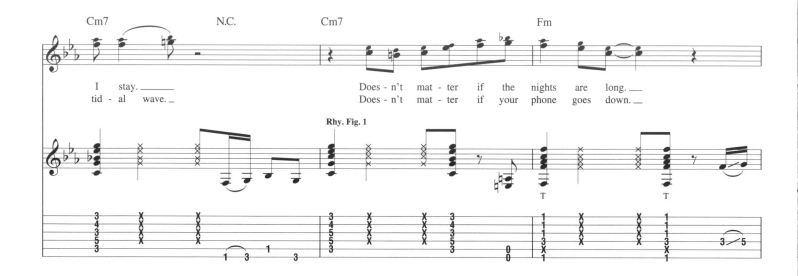

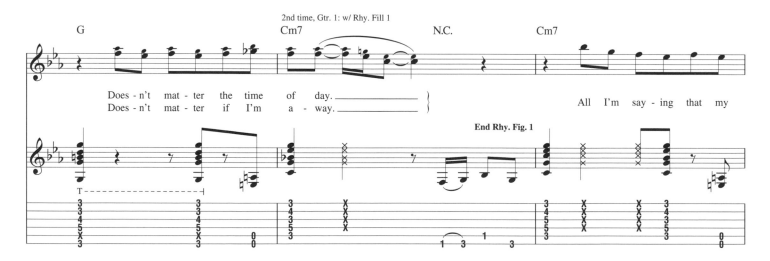

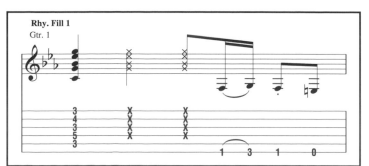

love is true, _____ I'm al - ways here for you. _____

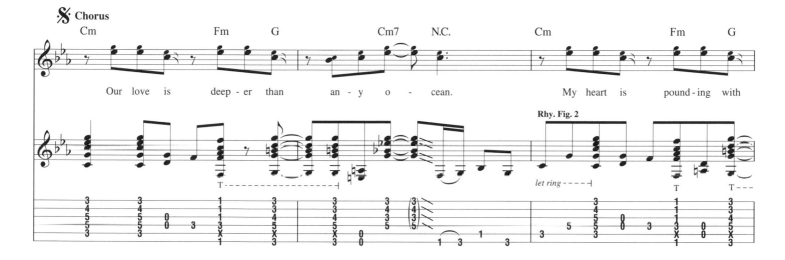

𝄋 Chorus

Our love is deep - er than an - y o - cean. My heart is pound - ing with

To Coda ⊕

real e - mo - tions.   Our love is   sweet - er than   an - y po - tion.

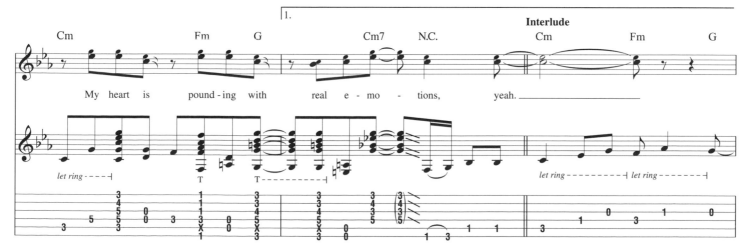

1. **Interlude**

My heart is pound - ing with real e - mo - tions, yeah. _____

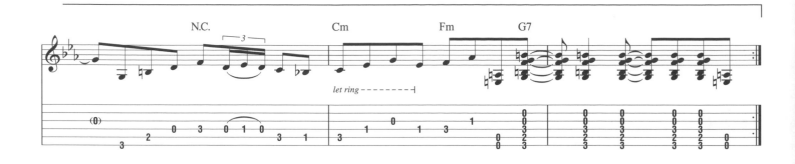

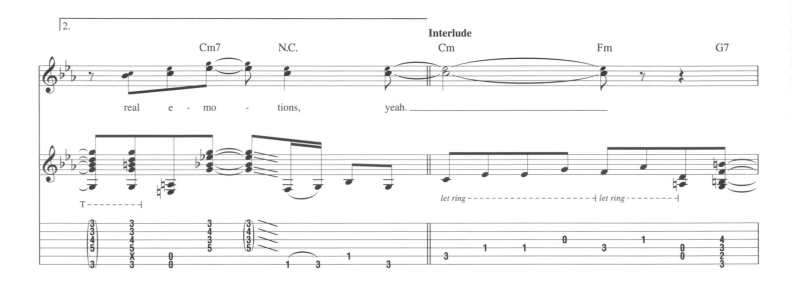

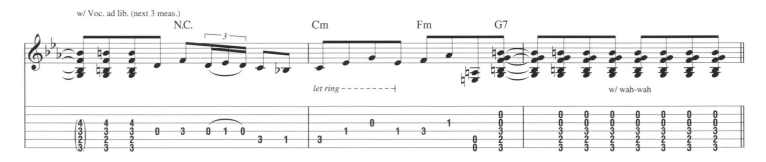

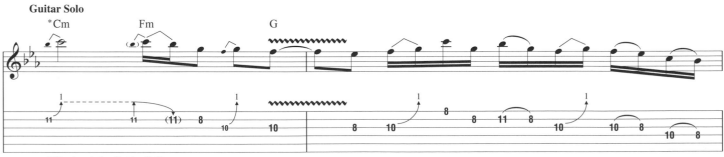

*Chord symbols reflect implied harmony.

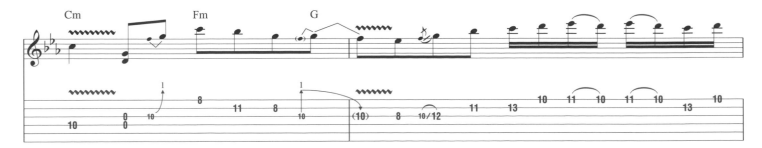

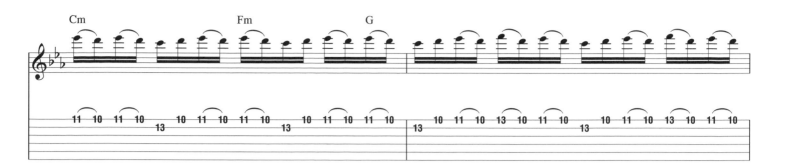

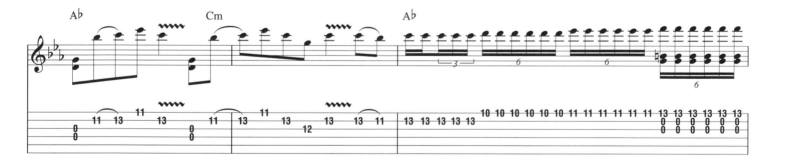

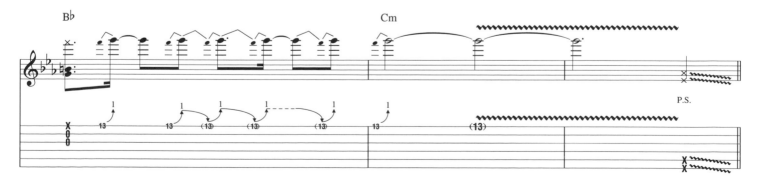

Bridge

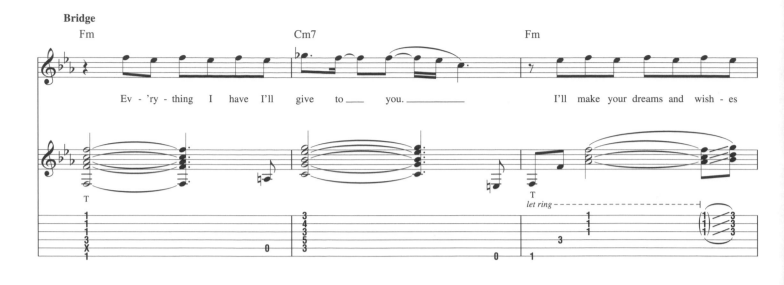

D.S. al Coda

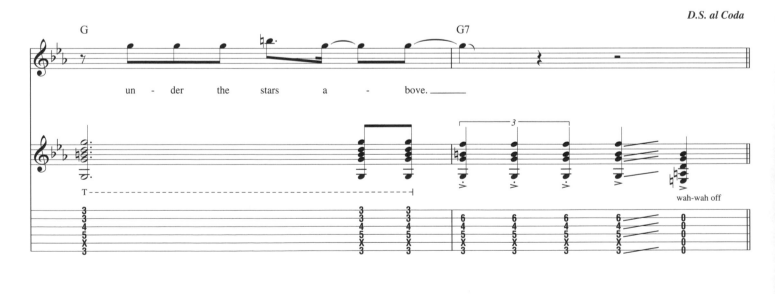

✪ Coda

an - y po - tion. My heart is pound-ing with real e - mo - tions, yeah.

Interlude

Yeah.

Gtr. 1

let ring

let ring

let ring

Outro-Guitar Solo

w/ wah wah

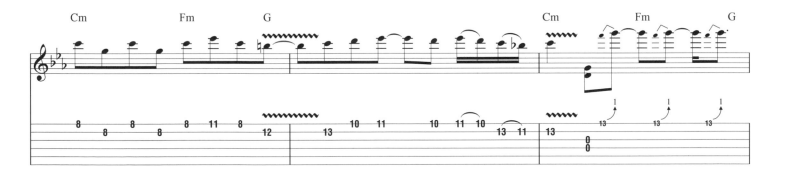

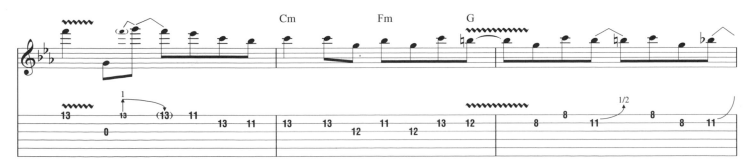

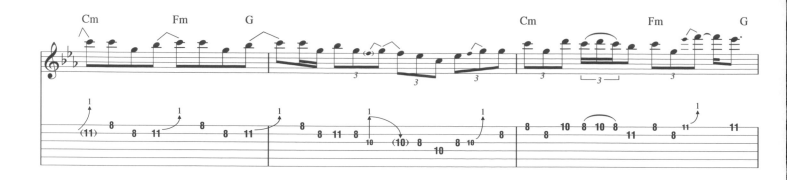

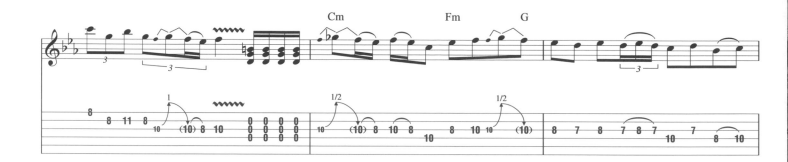

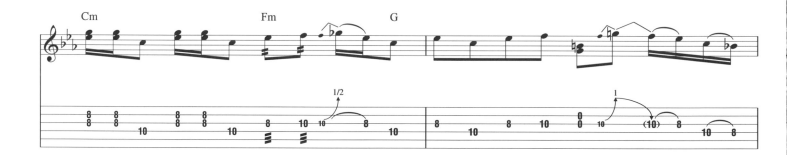

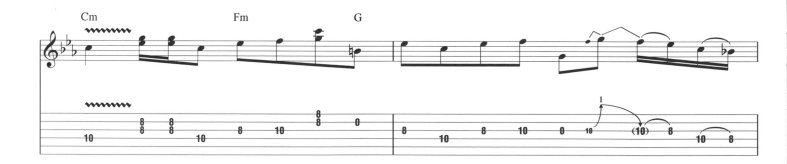

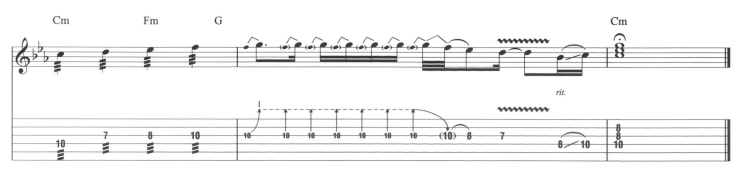

Tell Me Why

Words and Music by Henry Garza, Joey Garza, Ringo Garza and Phil Roy

Tune down 1/2 step:
(low to high) E♭-A♭-D♭-G♭-B♭-E♭

Intro
Moderately ♩ = 116

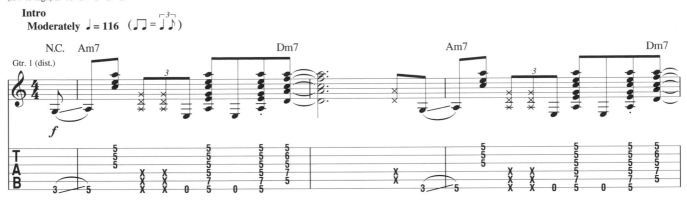

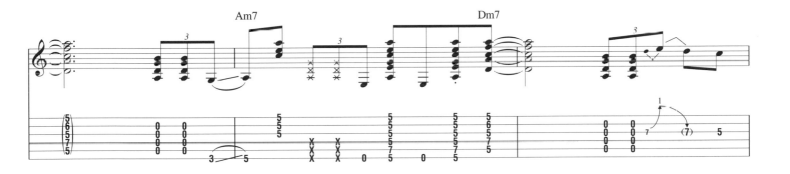

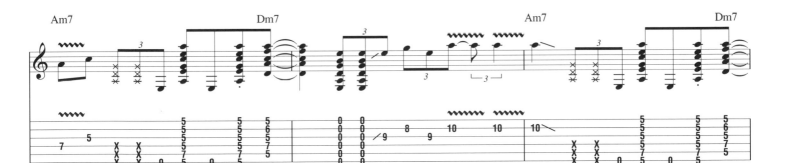

3rd time, Gtr. 1: w/ Fill 1

1. We've been to - geth - er for years, ____ you for me and me for
2. You nev - er act - ed like this, ____ you nev - er turned a - way ___
3. Por - qué te por - tas a - sí? ____ Por - qué me chas - tas men - ti -

you, my dear. ___ It seems you're chang - ing your song, ___
from my kiss. ___ Who am I with? I can't tell. ___
ras a ___ mí. ___ Me due - le men - to ha - con, ___

your tune is flat and all the words are wrong. _ 1., 2. Please tell me
Our life was good, but now it's some - thing else. __ 3. Di - me por -
me due - le mu - cho con la pas - sión. __

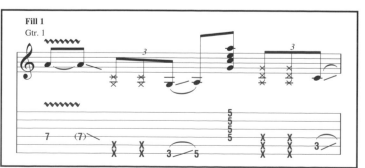

Fill 1
Gtr. 1

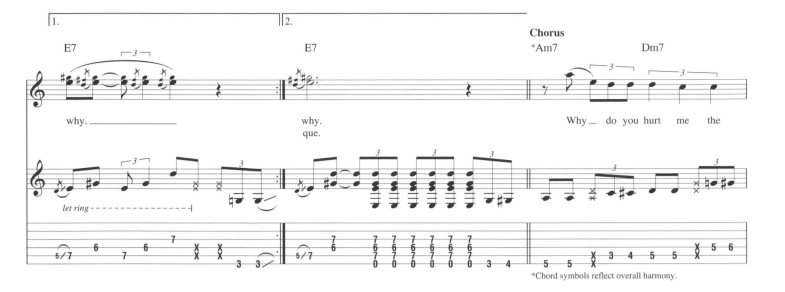

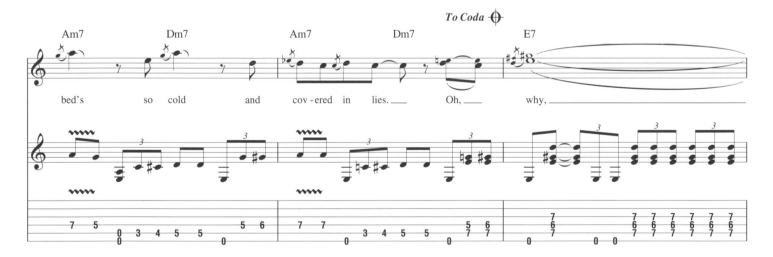

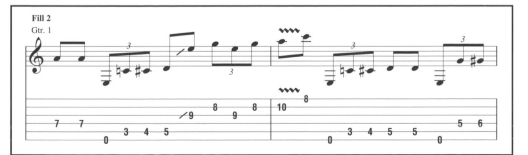

Guitar Solo

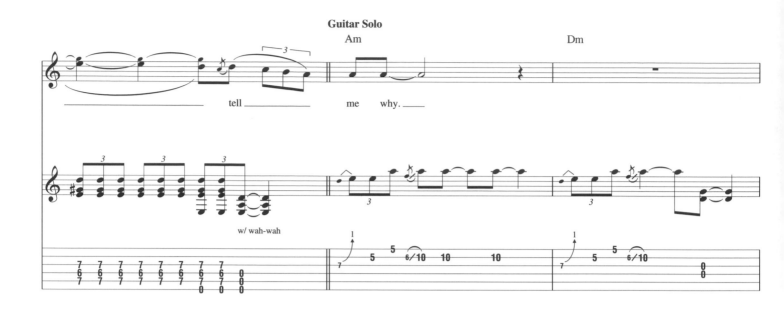

tell _____ me   why. _____

w/ wah-wah

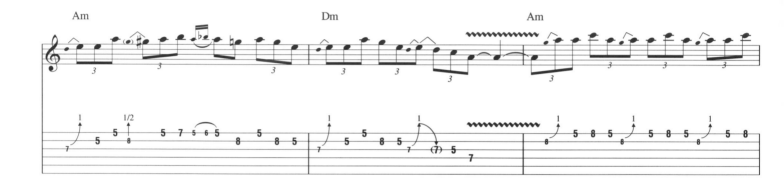

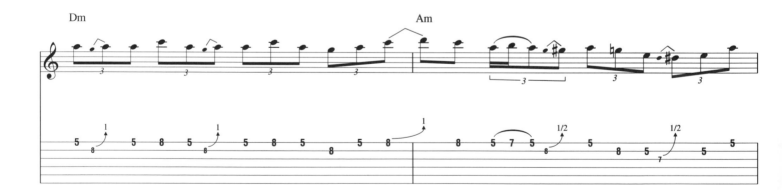

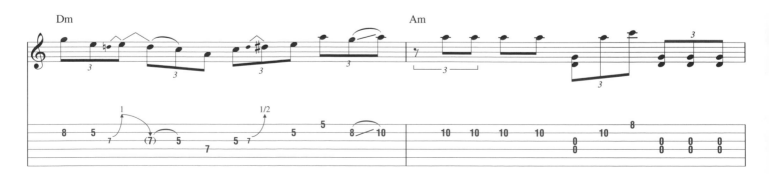

102

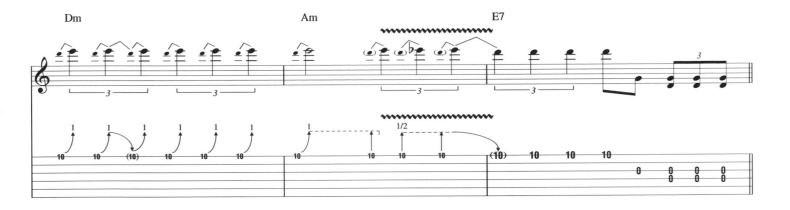

Organic Solo

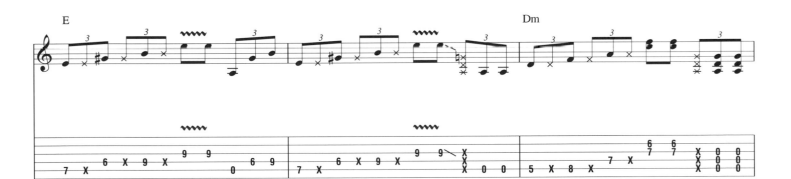

D.S. al Coda
(take 2nd ending)

◆ Coda

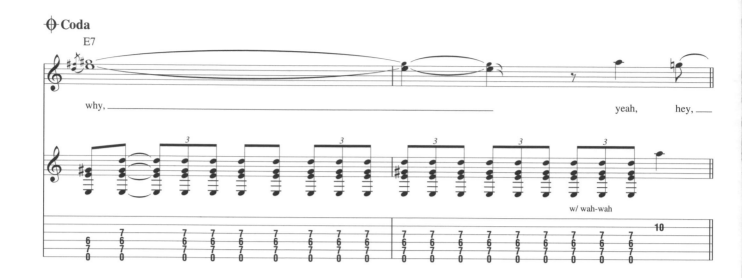

Outro-Guitar Solo

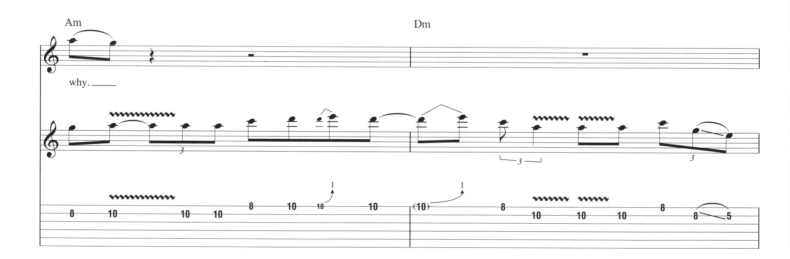

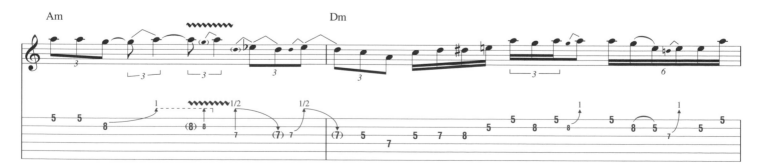

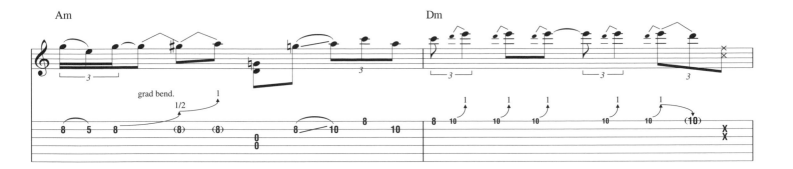

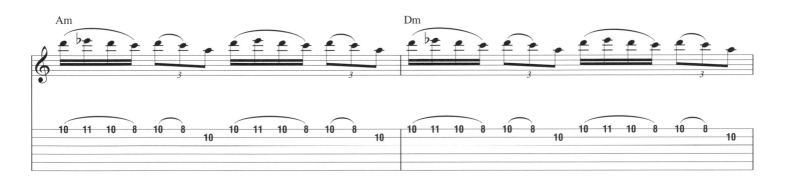

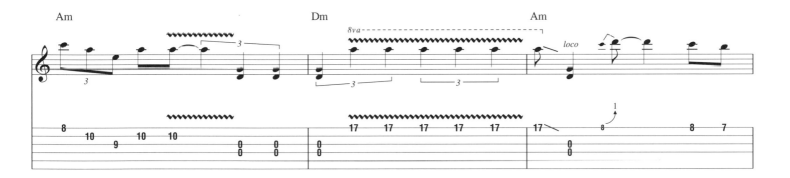

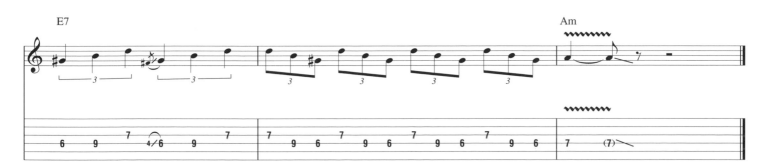

Velvet Sky

Words and Music by Henry Garza, Joey Garza, Ringo Garza and Kevin Wommack

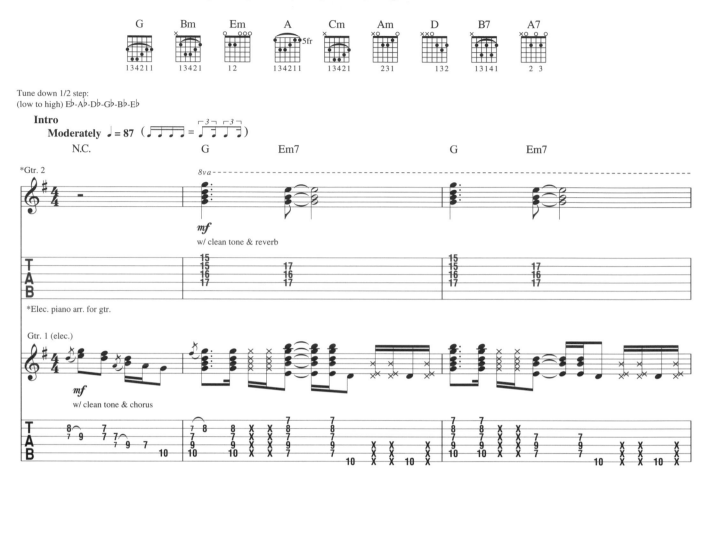

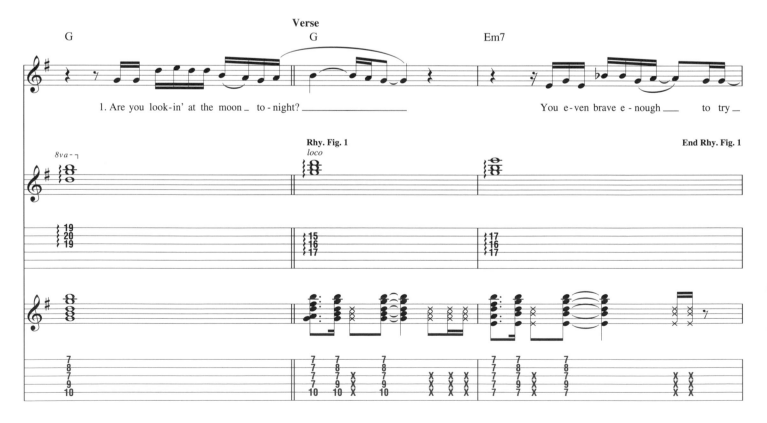

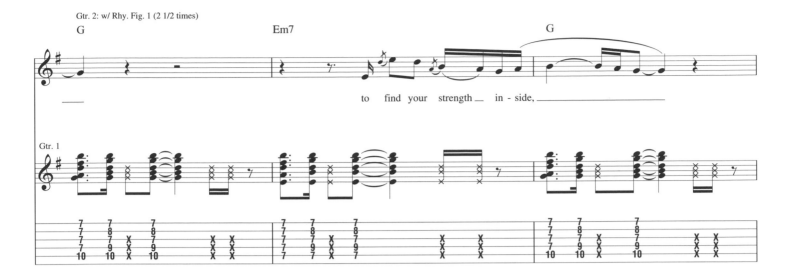

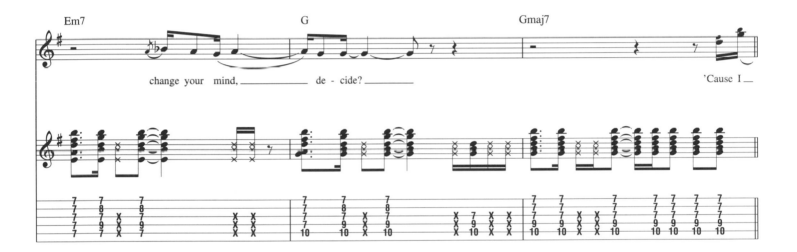

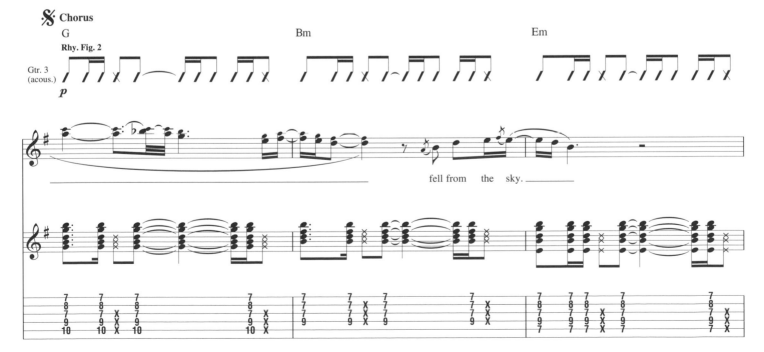

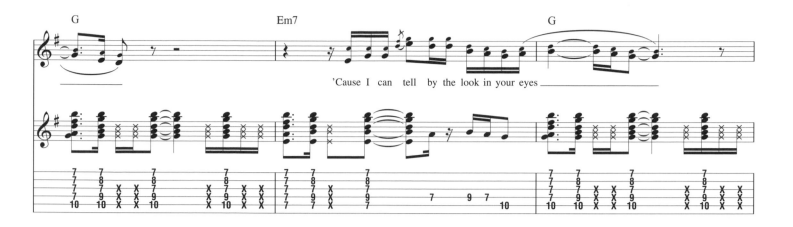

'Cause I can tell by the look in your eyes

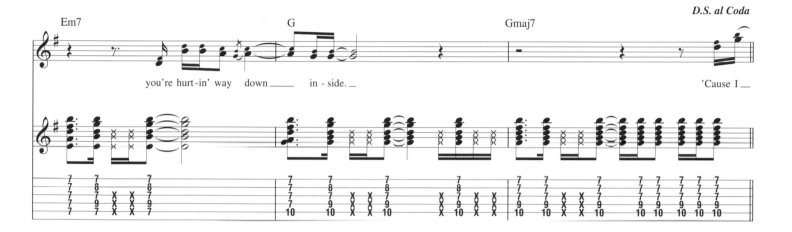

D.S. al Coda

you're hurt-in' way down ___ in - side. ___

'Cause I ___

◆ **Coda**

Guitar Solo
Gtr. 1: w/ Rhy. Fig. 3 (3 times)

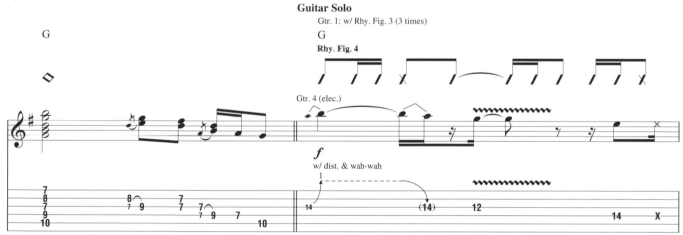

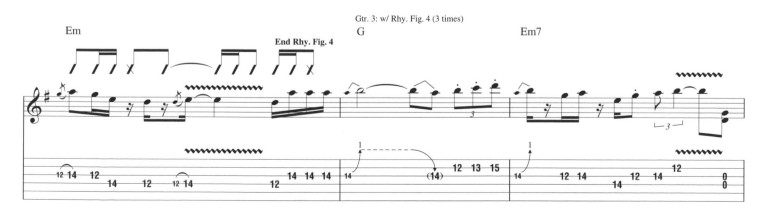

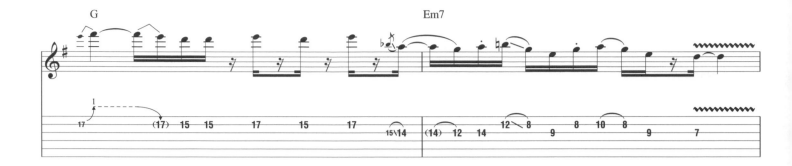

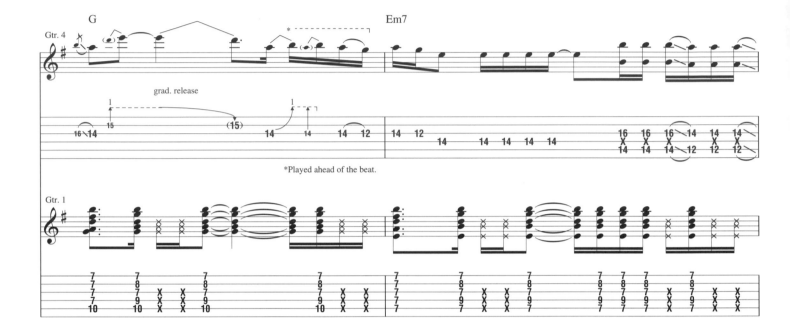

*Played ahead of the beat.

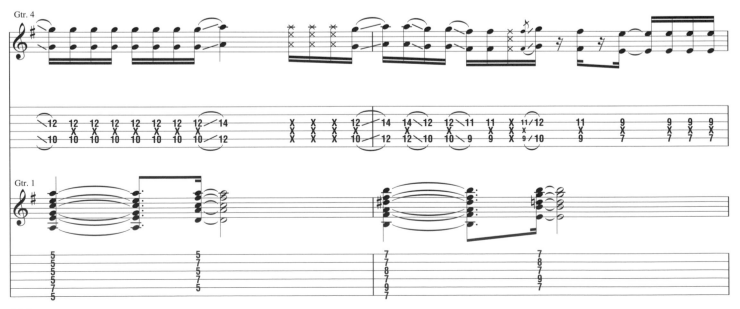

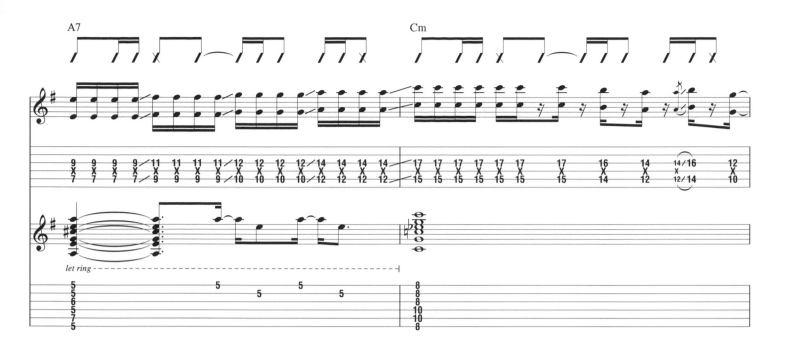

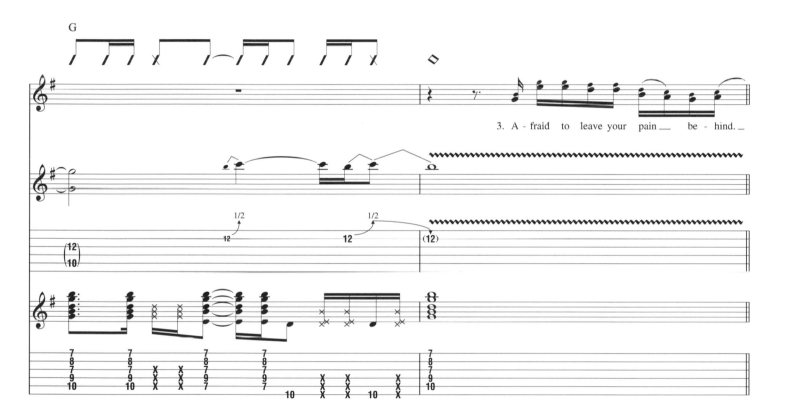

3. A - fraid to leave your pain __ be - hind. __

Verse
Gtr. 2: w/ Rhy. Fig. 1 (3 1/2 times)
Gtrs. 3 & 4 tacet

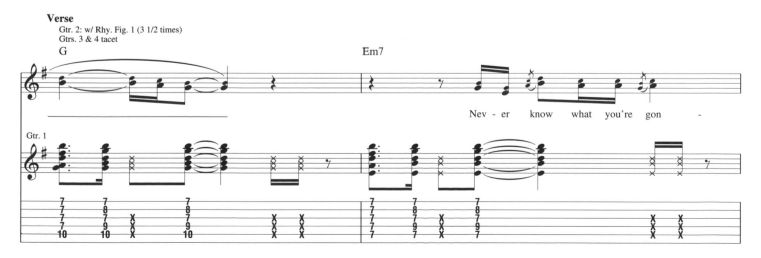

Nev - er know what you're gon -

Gtr. 1

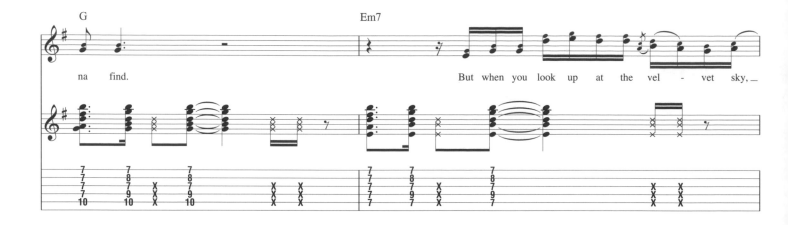

na find. But when you look up at the vel - vet sky, __

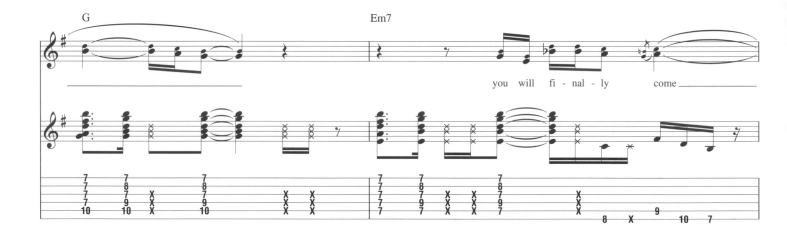

you will fi - nal - ly come __

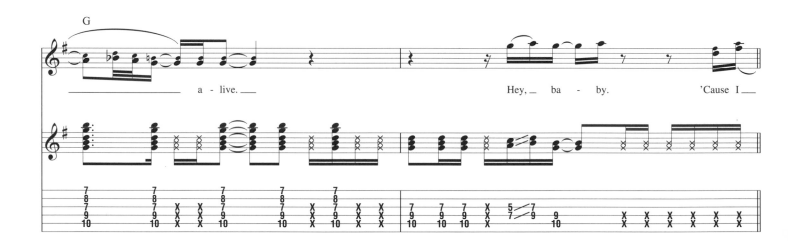

__ a - live. __ Hey, __ ba - by. 'Cause I __

Chorus
Gtr. 3: w/ Rhy. Fig. 2 (2 times)

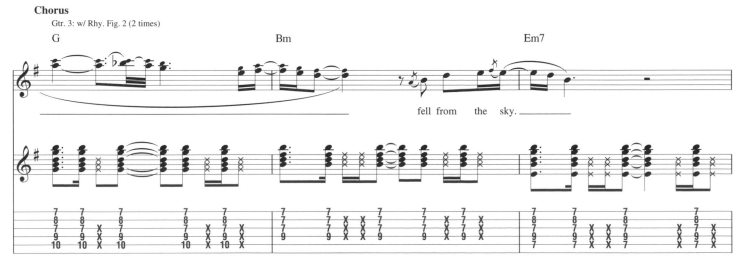

fell from the sky. __

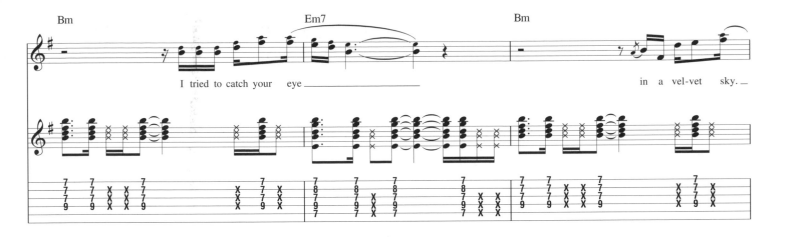

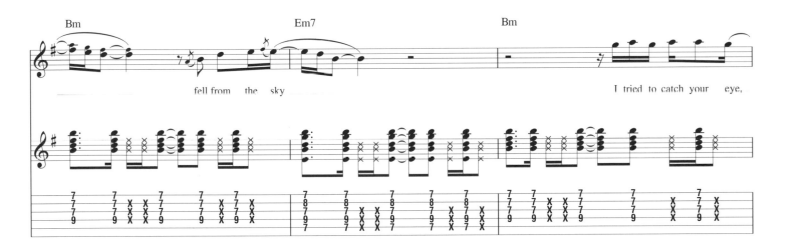

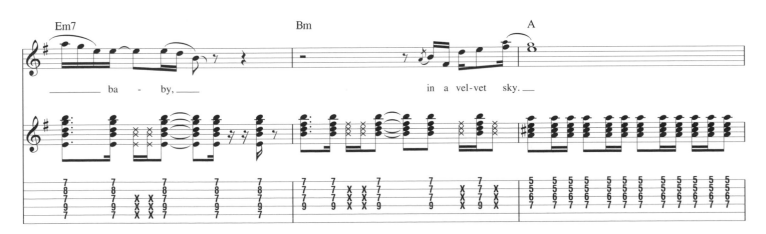

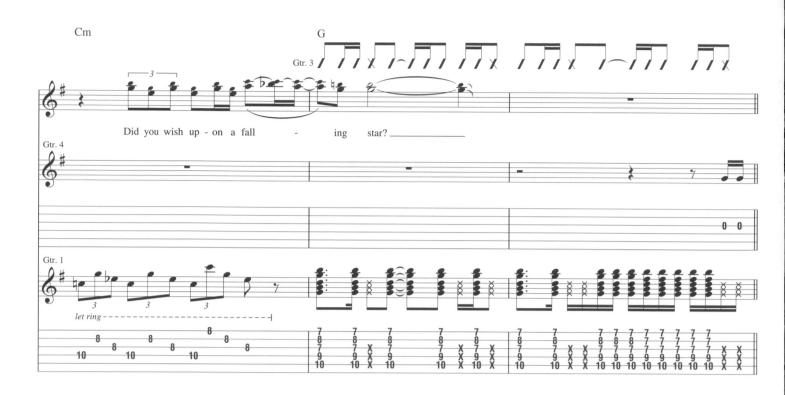

Did you wish up - on a fall - ing star? _____

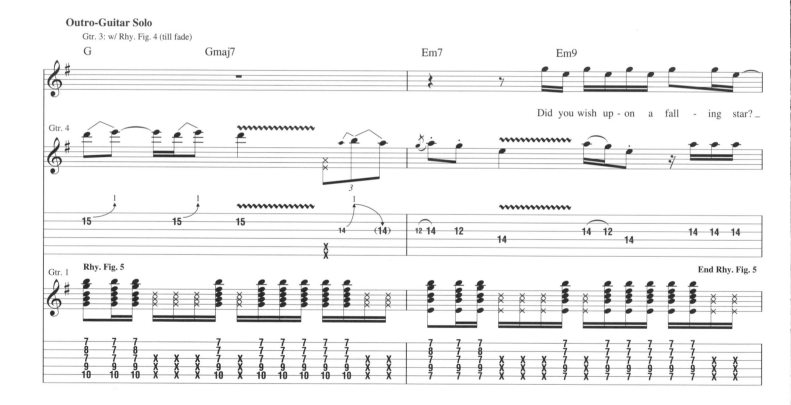

Outro-Guitar Solo

Did you wish up - on a fall - ing star? _

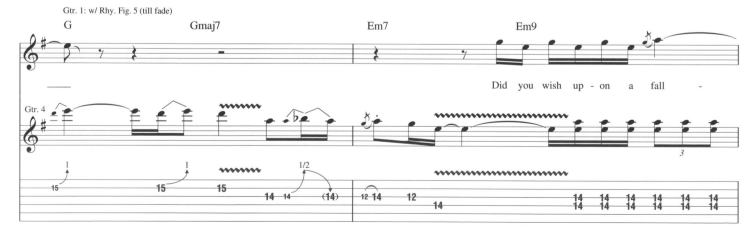

Did you wish up - on a fall -

-ing star? _____ Hey, __ ba - by, did you wish up-on a fall -

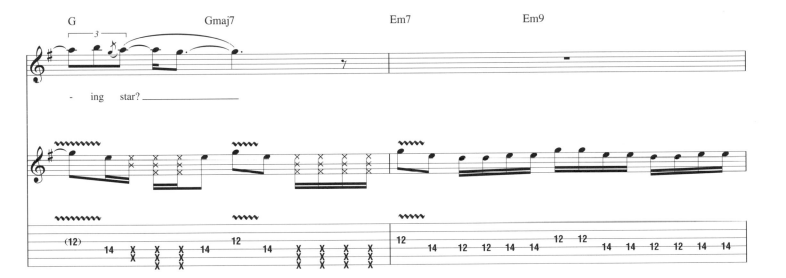

-ing star? _____

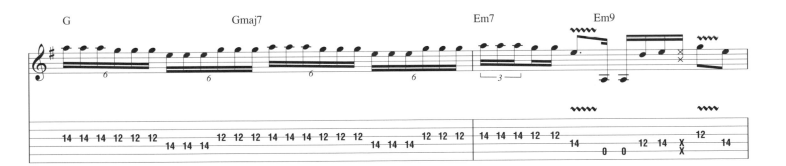

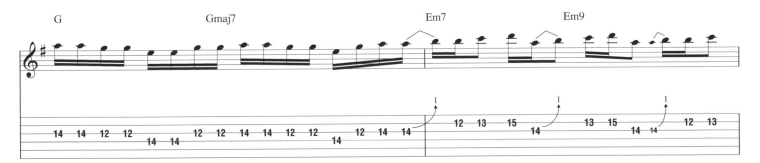

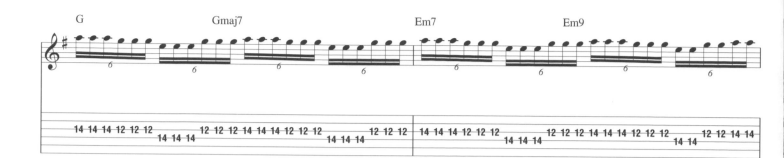

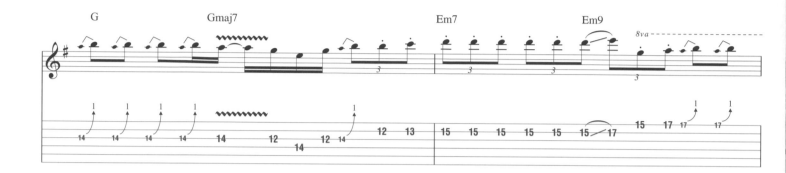

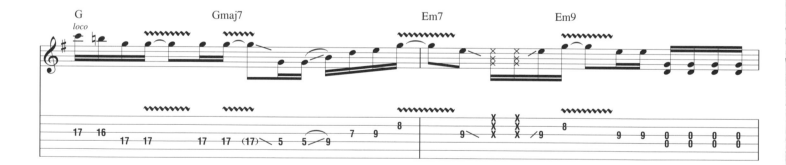

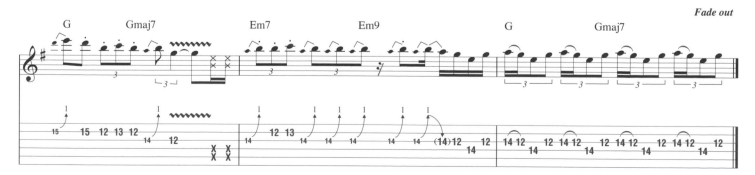

116

La Contestación

Words and Music by Henry Garza, Joey Garza, Ringo Garza and Jim Tullio

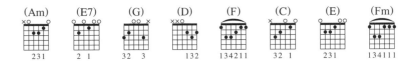

Gtr. 1: Tune down 1/2 step, capo II:
(low to high) E♭-A♭-D♭-G♭-B♭-E♭

Gtrs. 2 & 3: Tune down 1/2 step:
(low to high) E♭-A♭-D♭-G♭-B♭-E♭

*Piano arr. for gtr.   **Symbols in parentheses represent chord names respective to capoed guitar.
Symbols above represent actual sounding chords. Capoed fret is "0" in tab.
Chord symbols reflect overall harmony.

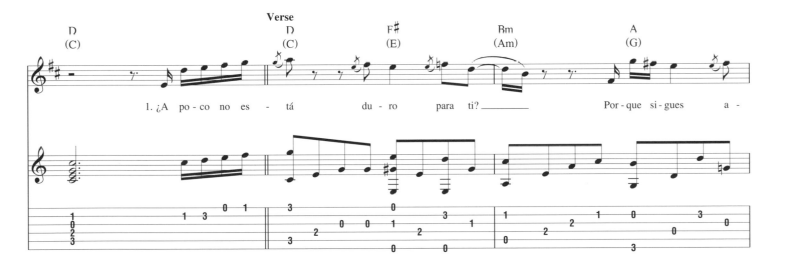

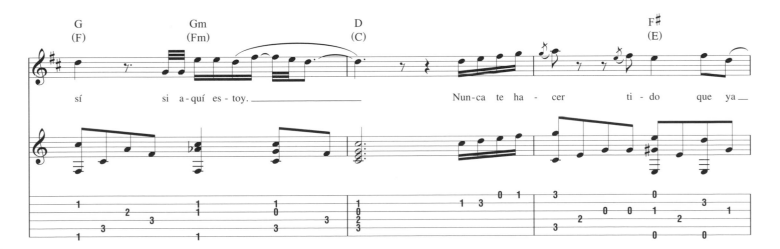

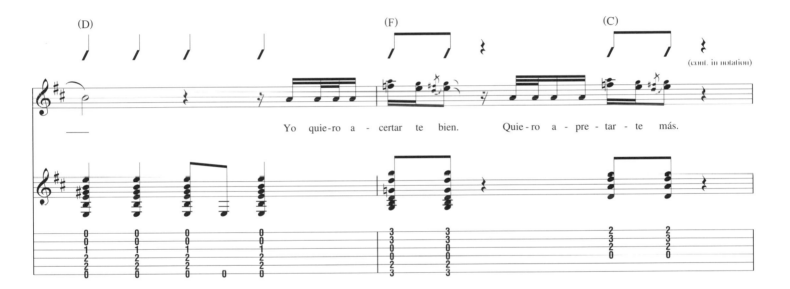

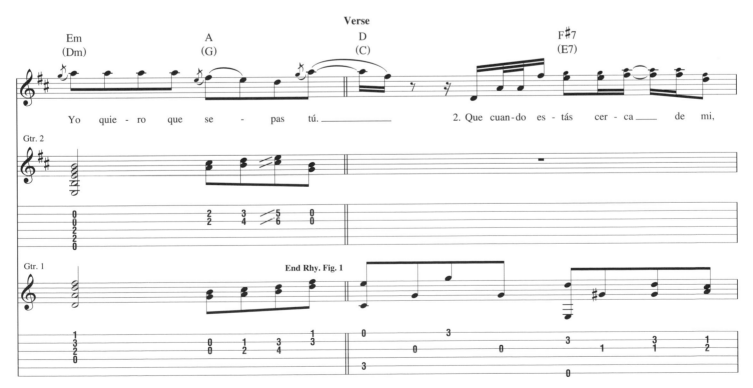

Ya no tien-es que llor-ar, por-que yo es-ta-ré a - llí.

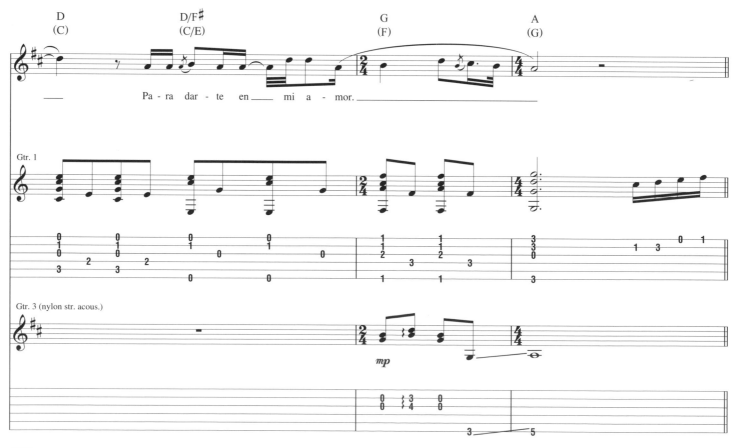

Pa-ra dar-te en mi a-mor.

Guitar Solo

Gtr. 3 tacet

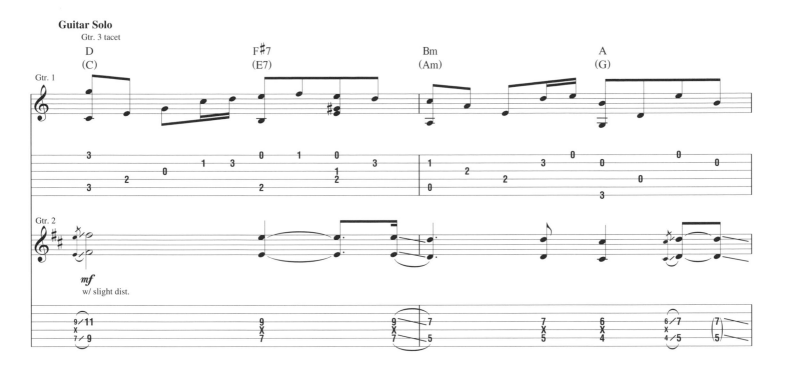

(cont. in slashes)

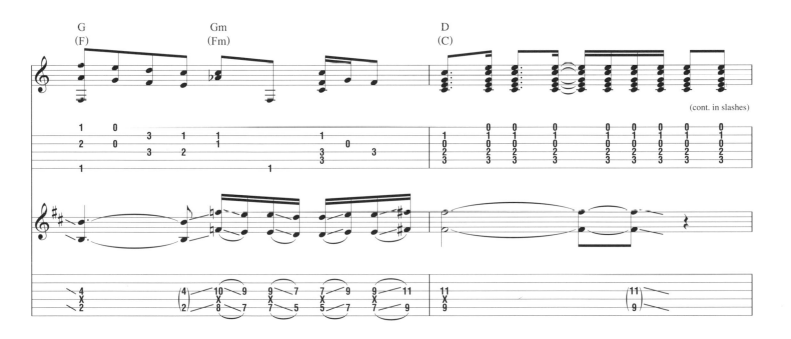

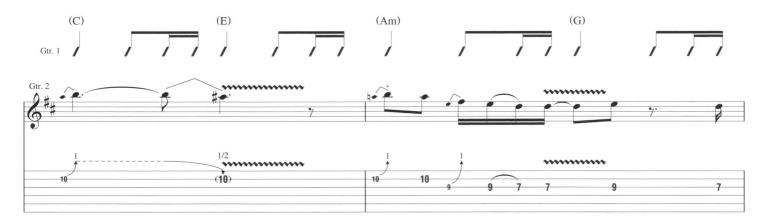

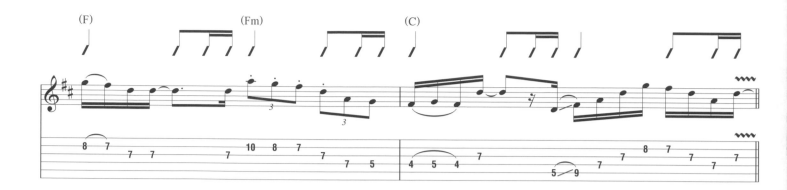

Chorus

Gtr. 1: w/ Rhy. Fig. 1

Que e - vi - ta, que____ no sien - tes.   Cuan -

do te ten - go cer - ca____ de mi._____   Yo quie - ro a -

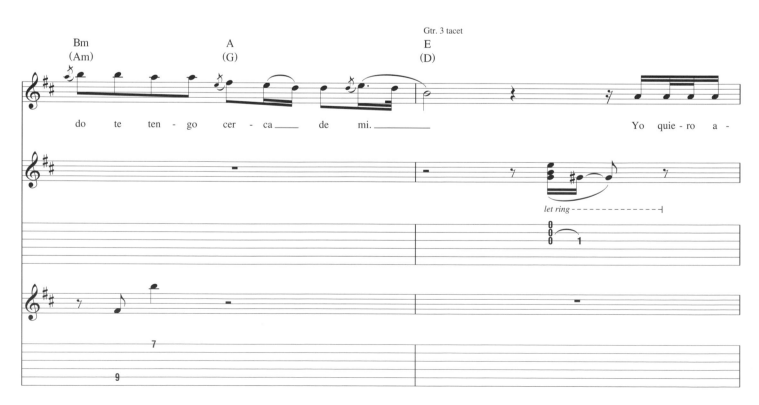

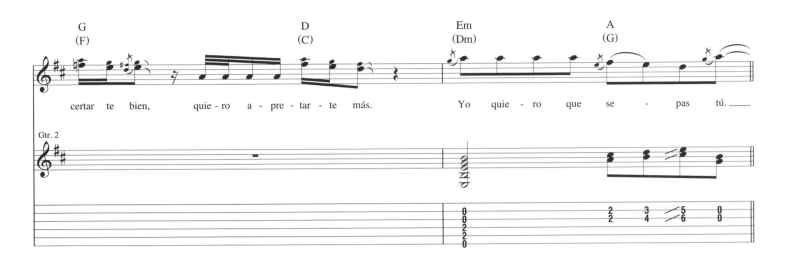

certar te bien, quie-ro a-pre-tar-te más.   Yo quie-ro que se - pas tú.

3. Que cuan-do es-tás cer-ca___ de mi,   Ya no tien-es que   llo-

rar, por-que yo es-ta-ré___ a-llí. _____   Pa-ra dar-te en___ mi a - mor.___

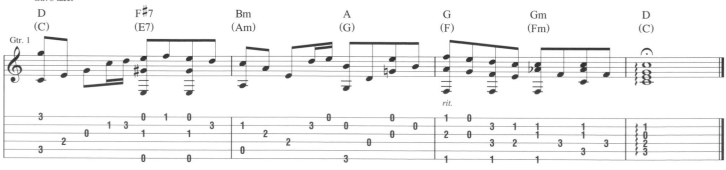

Guitar Notation Legend

Guitar Music can be notated three different ways: on a *musical staff*, in *tablature*, and in *rhythm slashes*.

RHYTHM SLASHES are written above the staff. Strum chords in the rhythm indicated. Use the chord diagrams found at the top of the first page of the transcription for the appropriate chord voicings. Round noteheads indicate single notes.

THE MUSICAL STAFF shows pitches and rhythms and is divided by bar lines into measures. Pitches are named after the first seven letters of the alphabet.

TABLATURE graphically represents the guitar fingerboard. Each horizontal line represents a a string, and each number represents a fret.

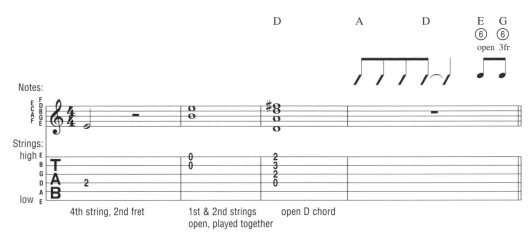

4th string, 2nd fret   1st & 2nd strings open, played together   open D chord

Definitions for Special Guitar Notation

HALF-STEP BEND: Strike the note and bend up 1/2 step.

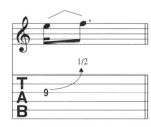

WHOLE-STEP BEND: Strike the note and bend up one step.

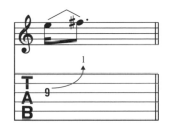

GRACE NOTE BEND: Strike the note and immediately bend up as indicated.

SLIGHT (MICROTONE) BEND: Strike the note and bend up 1/4 step.

BEND AND RELEASE: Strike the note and bend up as indicated, then release back to the original note. Only the first note is struck.

PRE-BEND: Bend the note as indicated, then strike it.

PRE-BEND AND RELEASE: Bend the note as indicated. Strike it and release the bend back to the original note.

UNISON BEND: Strike the two notes simultaneously and bend the lower note up to the pitch of the higher.

VIBRATO: The string is vibrated by rapidly bending and releasing the note with the fretting hand.

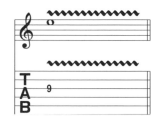

WIDE VIBRATO: The pitch is varied to a greater degree by vibrating with the fretting hand.

HAMMER-ON: Strike the first (lower) note with one finger, then sound the higher note (on the same string) with another finger by fretting it without picking.

PULL-OFF: Place both fingers on the notes to be sounded. Strike the first note and without picking, pull the finger off to sound the second (lower) note.

LEGATO SLIDE: Strike the first note and then slide the same fret-hand finger up or down to the second note. The second note is not struck.

SHIFT SLIDE: Same as legato slide, except the second note is struck.

TRILL: Very rapidly alternate between the notes indicated by continuously hammering on and pulling off.

TAPPING: Hammer ("tap") the fret indicated with the pick-hand index or middle finger and pull off to the note fretted by the fret hand.

NATURAL HARMONIC: Strike the note while the fret-hand lightly touches the string directly over the fret indicated.

PINCH HARMONIC: The note is fretted normally and a harmonic is produced by adding the edge of the thumb or the tip of the index finger of the pick hand to the normal pick attack.

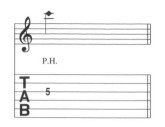

HARP HARMONIC: The note is fretted normally and a harmonic is produced by gently resting the pick hand's index finger directly above the indicated fret (in parentheses) while the pick hand's thumb or pick assists by plucking the appropriate string.

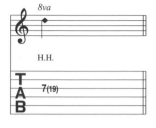

PICK SCRAPE: The edge of the pick is rubbed down (or up) the string, producing a scratchy sound.

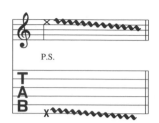

MUFFLED STRINGS: A percussive sound is produced by laying the fret hand across the string(s) without depressing, and striking them with the pick hand.

PALM MUTING: The note is partially muted by the pick hand lightly touching the string(s) just before the bridge.

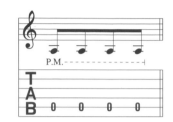

RAKE: Drag the pick across the strings indicated with a single motion.

TREMOLO PICKING: The note is picked as rapidly and continuously as possible.

ARPEGGIATE: Play the notes of the chord indicated by quickly rolling them from bottom to top.

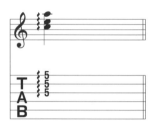

VIBRATO BAR DIVE AND RETURN: The pitch of the note or chord is dropped a specified number of steps (in rhythm) then returned to the original pitch.

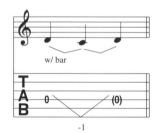

VIBRATO BAR SCOOP: Depress the bar just before striking the note, then quickly release the bar.

VIBRATO BAR DIP: Strike the note and then immediately drop a specified number of steps, then release back to the original pitch.

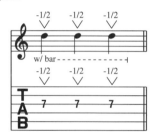

Additional Musical Definitions

(accent)	• Accentuate note (play it louder)	
(accent)	• Accentuate note with great intensity	
(staccato)	• Play the note short	
	• Downstroke	
	• Upstroke	
D.S. al Coda	• Go back to the sign (𝄋), then play until the measure marked "***To Coda***," then skip to the section labelled "**Coda**."	
D.C. al Fine	• Go back to the beginning of the song and play until the measure marked "***Fine***" (end).	

Rhy. Fig.	• Label used to recall a recurring accompaniment pattern (usually chordal).
Riff	• Label used to recall composed, melodic lines (usually single notes) which recur.
Fill	• Label used to identify a brief melodic figure which is to be inserted into the arrangement.
Rhy. Fill	• A chordal version of a Fill.
tacet	• Instrument is silent (drops out).
	• Repeat measures between signs.
1. 2.	• When a repeated section has different endings, play the first ending only the first time and the second ending only the second time.

NOTE: Tablature numbers in parentheses mean:
1. The note is being sustained over a system (note in standard notation is tied), or
2. The note is sustained, but a new articulation (such as a hammer-on, pull-off, slide or vibrato begins), or
3. The note is a barely audible "ghost" note (note in standard notation is also in parentheses).